Published by GLOWING LIGHT LTD 2021

SEEING BEYOND 2020 VISION
Soft Cover. July 2021.
Copyright © 2021 Peter Koren.
ISBN: 978-0-473-58522-8
Written by Peter Koren.
GLOWING LIGHT LTD
Auckland, New Zealand.

Table of Contents

Introduction

This book is a collection of articles and thoughts that were released in 2020.

This will be a year that will be remembered in the history books of the future generations as a tipping point to where the world began to shift from world-wide calamity, a heavily contested and critical election in the USA, riots and wars between opposing camps, which from the natural viewpoint is a very chaotic state of disaster, as declared in too many places due to the man-made pandemic created in the lab. We need to see what has been made in Heaven and from where the reality can be seen as a war between opposing Kingdoms being thrashed out in the hearts and minds of men and women on the globe; violently thrusting ideals on society, while behind the mask there is something sinister going on in the shadows.

If you are operating from a 2020 vision humanistic viewpoint then you will be limited to how you perceive the foundational fabric of things, such as what is truth and what is opposing the truth, these lines will be blurred when you are looking at the battle from a ground level line of sight vision. To really know what is happening behind the great stage of life on this earth, you will need insight from above and wisdom how to implement proper change based on righteous values.

We all need to be taken higher in the spirit with an eagle's vantage point, this is where the bigger picture can be viewed with clarity and we will no longer get wrapped up in the details that can be confusing and easily manipulated to represent a point of view that has an agenda attached to it.

Seeing Beyond 2020 Vision takes the reader through this journey where we look into the disturbing events of 2020 that unfolded before our eyes and we had the feeling that something was wrong, we couldn't quite put your finger on it, but we knew that this virus and the other related events was really sick. Let's just take a look behind the news to see what's really going on here. This brings the reader to taking the lid off the swirling pot of lies and deception to see that there is a problem. But what do you do with that information?

Seeing Beyond 2020 Vision offers the reader another perspective, which is the solution to the problem. This is the Good News approach where wisdom from above makes the difference and gives us a hope for the future.

If all you have is knowing what is wrong with the world, then your outlook will be a cloud of despair, because you know that the forces that are controlling this world's events and the populations has a horrendous grip on the outcome, we are looking at 1984 on steroids.

When the reader gets to the chapter, Seeing Beyond 2020 Vision, their hopes will be raised with renewed vision like the eagle and the view is like Heaven on Earth. But this book doesn't end here, there are more chapters that continue to reveal more details and more pieces of the puzzle are revealed, as well as the bright outlook Seeing Beyond 2020 Vision, so let this vision take you there.

Take the leap of faith, renew your mind and allow your sanctified imagination to see things out of this world, seeing beyond 2020 vision. This series of articles is now released in a format where you will see a progressive vision and then a victorious solution, followed by an elevated vision seeing beyond 2020 to a brighter future.

This is the answer, this is the Good News about Jesus Christ who has saved mankind from destruction, see beyond 2020 vision, you will be eternally thankful, filled with love, hope and endless joy.

Chapter 1

2020

Let's imagine just for a moment if you will, that parallel universes do exist and time travel is possible and inter dimension activity is infiltrating our space time material universe.

We need a reality in our lives that provides stability and allows us to navigate our future into 2020 and beyond. Clear visibility and eagle eye perspectives to take us through the changes rapidly overtaking us, in these strange shape shifting days. How can we discover what is the truth, while all of the wild theories are buzzing the airwaves of our times?

I see more insight coming and revelation as we get to know our Father and our Lord and Saviour more, as His Spirit leads us into more truth and shows us things to come.

Preparation for the times coming and the equipping of the saints is necessary to be an army arising, arrayed for the battle and the coming great harvest of souls. We are like dead bones being raised up in newness of life in the valley of dry bones.
Prophesy grace, grace to it

What are Parallel Possibilities?
Do Parallel Universes exist in the time space continuum?

This is a concept that is out there and it would mean that there is a whole other you living a parallel life almost like yours, but here is the thing, it is different because of choice.

There maybe one file that has this life and then there is another file with a whole different ball game.

I love the sci fi shows portraying these scenarios, I have watched them, whole seasons, lapped up the entire show, intrigued by the imaginative trips they take us on.

The thing with all of these imaginations, other dimensions and alternative realities, is that they do contain elements of what could be possible in an alternative existence. These theories do have an essence of reality, otherwise we would reject them as a far-fetched fantasy that has no connection to our imaginations. But an ounce of truth can also take us down an endless rabbit trail into oblivion, lost in space.

So what is the truth?

Your destiny is recorded before time began in the ether, describing the essence of you which is contained in the heavenly realms on a scroll.

You can choose your destiny or not discover it at all and just accept whatever comes your way good or bad.

Unlike fate where you are dealt the hand of how your life is going to be, faith requires your participation to bring what is recorded about your future possibilities into your reality.

You achieve your destiny by faith, not by passively accepting your fate!

Faith could be one file on you like a prophecy and fate could be the alternate file of how things will be that is imposed on you.
Fate is a bit like the stuff that happens to you and you just got to blooming well accept it. That is your lot! Just how it is and going to be! Or is it?
Faith is what elevates you above what fate has dished out to you.
This is a type of what the parallel universe is; on the one hand we have our destiny written on a scroll that can be fulfilled by faith as we choose this reality above what seems to be how it is.

Are you in the twist of fate?

Jesus came to give us life and life in abundance. The enemy comes to kill steal and destroy that life and he uses like a fate to fix us into a destination, which is the stuff that happens to us, where we came from, our environment, the influences, the authorities that shape and affect our outcome.
Ephesians 1:11
In Him also we have obtained an inheritance, being predestined according to the purpose of Him who works all things according to the counsel of His will,

Speaking about a parallel possibility, we are actually are in two places at once.
Our Heavenly position of authority and the place we hold on earth, where we interact in the physical world with all of its dynamics and rules.

When we are stuck in the rut of life, we need to access our alternative possibility,
It may appear initially just as a dream.

Ephesians 2:10
For we are His workmanship, created in Christ Jesus for good works, which God prepared beforehand that we should walk in them.

The Coming Third Temple Reformation.
What is it?
Is it a building, a structure, or a construct?
We are not made of concrete and we are not another brick that looks like all of the other bricks, except that we are made of the same stuff and can receive substance that makes us alive and full of purpose and hope, remember we are receive power from on high, but are also motivated to works by the Love of God.

In the Book of Revelation which reveals our Lord Jesus Christ, who is our substance of what really makes us to be.

There are letters written by the Apostle John, as he was in Heaven hearing the words of our Lord Jesus Christ for the seven churches of Asia in that time, who were shining like candles in a dark place.

The letters are relevant for the Church today and are warnings about what can cause us to lose our light, as we need to remain in Him to be a true light shining in the world.

Let's see if there are any similar things happening today that we need to pay attention to:

Losing our First Love

Having a reputation of being alive, but are in reality dead.

Tolerating a Jezebel spirit of witchcraft and control.

Being seduced into fornication and worshipping Idols.

The philosophy of the Nicolations overtaking our beliefs.

(Nicolations believed you could have a mixture of different beliefs, salvation comes from many different pathways and not just One Way as in Jesus is the Way, the Truth and the Life).

Lastly we have the warning of the Luke Warm Church, neither hot nor cold, basically ending up blind of our true heart condition, thinking we are rich, but in reality we are spiritually poor.

The Reformation.

Corresponds to the Temple restoration and rebuilding.

Destruction to the temple of God – could be the Church institutionalised by Man-made Government control.

Loss of the Early Church Faith

We read *"Contend for the Faith"* in the Book of Jude being a real challenge to hold fast.

Cessationism – the gifts and signs following believers were only for the 12 Apostles, not for the Church, we have the theory we need to live with just that.

Captivity of the church, being like the Israelites taken away into captivity by the Babylonians to a strange land.
Return from Captivity is like the Reformation, where faith is restored, *the just shall live by faith and we are saved by grace, not by our own works.*

Martin Luther and the voices of the Reformation could be a type of Zerubbabel, who was the Priest of the Lord during the rebuilding of the Temple, spoken about in the Book of Zechariah. The instruction from the prophet was *"Not by might or by power but by My Spirit the mountain will be removed"*.
We can Speak to the Mountain of opposition to our faith.
Like in Ezekiel's valley of dry bones, we can prophesy to what is dead in our lives and what doesn't line up with what God says about our lives.
There is a lot of shaking and rattling going on until things are established, as in Heaven so it is on earth.

Soul Gaps.
These missing pieces are like stolen treasures from our true image.
We need like a Defragmentation Therapy
Here is a scenario or a picture of what may be.
What if we are assigned our very own star in the universe?
We shine like a unique dazzling colourful star.

So what if we are given a star as an expression of us.

But if our soul has been hijacked by the thief of our destiny, then perhaps this star has been overlapped by darkness and the ruling and reigning features are stolen.

This star and all of its shining features and now utilised for dark purposes.

Don't let the enemy of your soul rob you of your inheritance and blessings.

Ephesians 1:3

Blessed be the God and Father of our Lord Jesus Christ, who has blessed us with every spiritual blessing in the heavenly places in Christ,

Isaiah 40:26

Lift up your eyes on high, and behold who hath created these things, that bringeth out their host by number: he calleth them all by names by the greatness of his might, for that he is strong in power; not one faileth.

Be encouraged to take your place in life, to be seated above the adversities of life and the voices that tell you that you are not good enough.

Take hold of the hem of the garment of Jesus. Press through the crowd and don't miss out on your blessings, that will take you to where you belong in Christ Jesus, you are seated with Him in the Heavenly Realms.

Psalm 103:6

The Lord executeth righteousness and judgment for all that are oppressed.

This verse tells us that God is looking out for the oppressed, those who are under it, missing out on life and being dictated to by the cruel systems. God will bring His Judgement on those oppressors that rule over us and keep us bound. Most of all, it is God who declares us Righteous and accepted by the blood of Jesus and the work of the cross, we can by faith enter into the place of justice, where God is the just judge representing us, Jesus is our advocate and is setting us free, cancelling our debts.

We are blessed so that we can be a blessing to others and tell them the Good News of Hope and a Future.
This is your possible reality.

It is there, it exists, it may not look like it, but it is True.
It is yours by faith, take a hold of it.

Vision of 2020, can you see it now?

Chapter 2

Within our Sphere

It is best for us to discover our sphere of influence and rise up within what has been appointed for us to be and do in life.
That's where the power is.
That's where our source is.
That's where faith arises to overcome obstacles and achieve our unique greatness.
That's where our creativity flourishes.
That's where the provision is.
That's where our dreams and our vision will become crystal clear.
That's where our talents shine.
That's where you are really you.
The best you possible.
I am the real me!

Where our impossible becomes possibilities.
We are the authentic you and me!
2 Cor. 10:13
[13] We, however, will not boast beyond measure, but within the limits of the sphere which God appointed us-a sphere which especially includes you. NJKV
Psalm 16
[5] The Lord is the portion of mine inheritance and of my cup: thou maintainest my lot.
[6] The lines are fallen unto me in pleasant places; yea, I have a goodly heritage.

What then is our sphere?
It is who and what we are meant to be.
It is how the LORD imagines us to be and sees
us doing.

We just are because we inherited these qualities
within our DNA and when we find our lot in life,
it is the most pleasant place to be. Life is
fulfilling, how it should be.
Why?
Psalm 139
*14 I will praise You, for I am fearfully and
wonderfully made;*
Marvelous are Your works,
And that my soul knows very well.
15 My frame was not hidden from You,
When I was made in secret,
*And skillfully wrought in the lowest parts of the
earth.*
*16 Your eyes saw my substance, being yet
unformed.*
And in Your book they all were written,
The days fashioned for me,
When as yet there were none of them.

The book of secrets revealed.
This is the book that describes the real you and
me, even when things are not happening as
intended.
What! The pages written coming to pass in our
lives.
What is written has substance, we can have
faith, it is a given God kind of faith, because it is
the substance of things hoped for when not yet
seen.

When we are in.
"I am in!" - you can feel it!
What are you?
Artist, Business Owner, Musician, Architect,
Fashion Designer, Engineer, Mechanic, Pilot,
Evangelist, Prophet, Caregiver, Homemaker.
What it is your sphere of influence? You belong
there!
Why it is not!
Generational corrupted DNA.
Life distractions.
Circumstances.
The cruelty of life.
Disappointments.
Losing sight of who we really are.
Blindness.

When we do need to apply eye salve, as we can't
really see?
We can purchase eye salve, apply the healing
properties, like highly refined and pleasant
essential oils. The anointing that destroys yokes
holding us from where and who we are meant to
be, we need to purchase it, which means to go
after it, spend time and energy to take
possession of what belongs to us.

The Apostle Paul was blind and had scales on
his eyes.

Paul was originally known as Saul, he had a
different identity and name.
Paul was the greatest Apostle, but he didn't start
out that way.

He was killing people who were believers in Jesus.
He was working against the Church of Jesus Christ and was opposed to the Kingdom of God.

He was opposing Jesus who is Lord of all creation and the King of kings.
Paul was acting different to what was described in the pages of his book!

Yes, he had the passion and the zeal and was doing religious things and they had similarities to what was written about him. But, he was misdirected by a blindness to the truth and he was using his gifts for the wrong purposes in opposition to the Kingdom of God.

Paul's gifts became a tool in the hand of the enemy of God and caused destruction.
Therefore, Paul was knocked off his high and mighty, religious horse by a bright light and he was then literally blind and then Jesus revealed who He was and Paul then saw the error of his ways and he was saved and became the greatest Apostle.

As you can now see, you can become great even though you may have started out on the wrong track, you might have intentions to do well, but like Paul did when he was known as Saul, living against the plans and intentions of God.

One day as I was walking I saw a large dragonfly.

The dragonfly was a magnificent looking
creature, but it was dead, it was caught in a
fence wire like it was caged.
I noticed it had very big eyes.

What is this symbolically?

Sometimes we might have a big dragonfly
keeping us under surveillance by the enemy, so
that he can continue his influence over us,
knowing our movements, keeping us contained
within the box he has for us, where our talents
are used up by the enemy.

The enemy does not want us to come out of the
box, as it is like a prison keeping us under his
control. If we are trying to accomplish something
or get out of the rut, he can devise a plan to
knock us back down in the box. The enemy will
continue carrying out his schemes to keep us
locked into his plans for us.
You could be assigned a Surveillance Demon.

What I am seeing is the box of containment will
no longer hold you and the plans and
restrictions of the enemy will be destroyed.
You can now see.
Jesus came to destroy the works of the enemy.
The surveillance instrument will be eliminated,
blocked and remain stuck in a cage.

When you come out of the box of containment
you will receive eyes that can see who you really
are and your future not infected by your past.

From out of the box you will enter into the
sphere, the sphere is expansive and always
growing, it is not a container, it is a world full of
possibilities. You've heard of *"the world is your
oyster"*, there's a pearl of great price waiting for
you and has your name on it.
We could be Moulded into wrong thinking.
We can be shaped in the wrong ways.
Revert back to the original properties.
After conducting some research it has been
revealed that there exists shape memory
materials that can revert back into original form
after being bent and twisted out of shape.

We can be resilient.
Come back into Agreement with God how He
made you and sees you.
There can be re alignment.
Position yourself for success and allow Him to
redeem your time and energy as you bounce
back into shape.

Jesus encourages us to ask and keep on asking
until we receive.
This is the process of faith and persistence when
things are not seen, but are hoped for.
We have received the Holy Spirit, He is our guide
and counsellor.
He leads us into all truth.
He intercedes for us.
Praying in the Spirit helps for all things working
out for the good.

When we are abiding in the vine, we are
positioned and placed into the life source.

We are now in the ordained place of authority, to rule and reign in life and overcome.

We are in the sphere.
Then ask anything you desire and it shall be done for you. The substance becomes a reality.
John 15
7 If you abide in Me, and My words abide in you, you will ask what you desire, and it shall be done for you.
8 By this My Father is glorified, that you bear much fruit; so you will be My disciples.
9 "As the Father loved Me, I also have loved you; abide in My love.
10 If you keep My commandments, you will abide in My love, just as I have kept My Father's commandments and abide in His love."
Within our Sphere we get to do the greater works.
John 15
12 "Most assuredly, I say to you, he who believes in Me, the works that I do he will do also; and greater works than these he will do, because I go to My Father.
13 And whatever you ask in My name, that I will do, that the Father may be glorified in the Son.
14 If you ask anything in My name, I will do it.
John 15
16 You did not choose Me, but I chose you and appointed you that you should go and bear fruit, and that your fruit should remain, that whatever you ask the Father in My name He may give you.

John 15
23 "And in that day you will ask Me nothing. Most assuredly, I say to you, whatever you ask the Father in My name He will give you.
24 Until now you have asked nothing in My name. Ask, and you will receive, that your joy may be full.

Then truly we really are who we really are if you get the picture.

Read the book *(heavenly scroll)*; ask for it to be revealed to you, if things are still unclear.
Guess what this is God's will for us.
Within our sphere we become as He is so are we in the world. *1 John*
So how do we know what our sphere is? First of all we need to have the same mind, same thinking as our Father God - be connected as one with Him - *John 17*, two hearts are combined into one.
Co-heirs Co-labourers is two working as one on the same vision. Those who wait on God become united into His ways. Abiding in the vine is being connected and receiving the life source to produce the right fruit. We will be spending the time and energy to allow God to transform our thinking to see as He sees. *Romans 12* offering our bodies for His purposes, by allowing the infilling of the Holy Spirit. Praying in tongues, fasting, being with God in a relationship, so we are in true partnership with Him, He calls us His friends. Entering into His rest. Resting from our works to enter into His works in partnership.

Then our desires are fine-tuned and become
pure in motivation as well as coming from the
pages of our book, because we are taking time to
read them and see who we are each day and
where we are going, putting aside our agendas
and how we think the universe should be run.
Aligning.
Becoming a pure channel.
Having no mixtures of beliefs.
No opposing directions.
The ox is moving in the right direction, has the
yoke on that directs the feet in the right
direction.
Quantum physics.
Hidden Energy.
Jesus created all things and is holding all things
together.
When we tap into who we are in Him - abiding in
Him.
We can ask what we desire and it shall be so.
As the hidden energy will create our future and
move things into place in the physical world to
align with Gods will being done on earth.
Voice activation is a big part of creating our
world which is the sphere of influence we are
given as Kings and Priests of Royalty.
Seated with Him in the Heavenly realms.
We are seated there for a reason to rule and
reign with Him.
And Jesus is the connection and the Holy Spirit
empowers us to move Heaven to Earth.

People of faith framed their world. Hebrews.
Faith people created their future based on faith
in the unseen possibilities.

From the quantum positions of all possible scenarios, is our rightful place and future, we are co-creators in this.

Those who wait on the Lord.
Will rise up like the eagle *Isaiah 40.*
Renew strength - gain energy to rise above and be positioned in authority.
See with a new perspective as God sees the world from above.
Be seated in the Heavenly realms and know that you are there in confidence.
Actuality and fullness is possible.
The process is waiting on the Lord, the effect is mounting up rising above the weights of sin and the influences of the world with renewed strength to take your place within the sphere of influence that God has gifted you with and given freely with the grace gifting to achieve it.

We will be about doing the Fathers business and keeping the Fathers commandments by being representatives for Jesus on earth. Look for Love Joy and Peace and then you know you are on the right path.

Ephesians 2:10
[10] *For we are His workmanship, created in Christ Jesus for good works, which God prepared beforehand that we should walk in them.*

Ephesians 4:15,16
[15] *but, speaking the truth in love, may grow up in all things into Him who is the head-Christ-*

16 from whom the whole body, joined and knit together by what every joint supplies, according to the effective working by which every part does its share, causes growth of the body for the edifying of itself in love.

We all got a place and an essential part to play. The body needs all of the different parts, it can't function fully by just having one or two heroes that everyone else is dependent on.
We are all unique, we are not a copy of someone else famous, or someone we admire, or someone we envy.
No! We are all a necessary person, when we enter into our sphere of influence we can be the game changers and not be the one that is under the systems of the world and the cunning schemes of man's agendas for others to be under their control.

The truth is all about Jesus and who we are in Him.
He is the way the truth and the life!
Jesus came to dismantle the works of the enemy in our lives and establish who we really are.
Jesus says to you, *"come up here and sit with Me where I rule in the heavenly realms.*
You can rule with Me, I need you to take your place and make a difference for Me on earth as it is in Heaven."
Ephesians 1:11
11 In Him also we have obtained an inheritance, being predestined according to the purpose of Him who works all things according to the counsel of His will,

We all are a story to be told, written on the pages of our life story in a book made especially for you and me, every page has a wonderful day created to perfection, waiting for us to enter into, to be and do the greater works.
Just be You!

What if you are called to be a Kingdom Entrepreneur? What does it mean? You are called like Joseph with administrative brilliance and foresight to manage finances on a National level effecting international outcomes, you can dream big.
Or like King Solomon, having wisdom to generate wealth with creativity and technology, the nations will marvel and come to you for advice on how to create economic boom time, gold in abundance and silver lining the streets.
Or you might be like Isaac he prospered in the time of famine, truly a miracle worker of God. What does it mean when you are abiding in the vine and Jesus is Lord and the CEO over your company gains? Money hasn't got you, you have money as a resource, it means you are a trustworthy steward for the Kingdom of God. Abraham was blessed with extravagant possessions, money didn't possess him, he was trusted with the possession of money and was ruling and reigning as a friend of God, he was blessed to be a blessing. What does that mean? Millions and Billions poured into the Kingdom of God for the purposes of a Billions Soul Harvest. It means His will being done on earth and His Kingdom come in the Billions.

Be blessed, Gods will is that you prosper, as
your soul prospers in the right heart attitude
and having the capacity for great faith. There is
a river flowing, if we are in the groove we can
steward great harvest blessings to multitudes in
the valley of decision.

Be the world changer He made you to be.
Within our sphere we can see for miles from our
mountaintop.
Within our sphere we are living from the
mountaintop.
Within our sphere with the help of Jesus we can
be the best.
Within our sphere we have inoculation from
disease, pestilences and plagues, including a
deadly strain of a virus.

I may not have arrived, things can look far away
in the distance and the obstacles are looming
over me.
But, as long as I have vision.
As long as I have purpose.
As long as I have breathe and I know God loves
me.
My past was shaped by the downturn currents
of this world, but my future is framed to form by
faith what is written about me within my sphere,
which already exists outside the constraints of
the clocks of decay.
My future is preordained by the creative
enterprises of God waiting for activation into the
now.
I am on my way within my sphere.

Romans 8:13

[13] For if you live according to the flesh you will die; but if by the Spirit you put to death the deeds of the body, you will live.

The flesh is what we are not supposed to be and doing.

How do we put to death the deeds of the flesh by the Spirit?

From the following verses in *Romans 8*, comes the answers.

Be led by His Spirit - Holy Spirit leads us into all truth and shows us things to come.

Operate in faith not fear.

Be adopted as His son and daughter and know you are accepted in the beloved.

Be a co-heir with Christ, enter into living by the Spirit and then you will be glorified together with Christ.

Within our sphere we are one with Him.

We are abiding in Him.

We are ruling and reigning in Life.

We have life and life in abundance.

Within our sphere, we are following Him into the plan that He has written on our scrolls.

We remain in love because He is love.

As He is so are we in this world.

Within our sphere, we are a city on the hill.

He is the Light to this world and He lights us up.

Within our sphere, His will be done.

Within our sphere, His Kingdom comes into our world.

Chapter 3

The Pyramid Scheme

The Pyramids are a marvel wonder of the world.
How were they constructed?
Who made them?
What are they for?

They stand as a monument to some of man's most outstanding achievements and engineering ingenuity.

Egypt what a mystery, is it science or religion, reaching to the cosmos, a connection to the gods?

Let's use our imaginations and know that as children of the Most High God and co-heirs with Christ, we can take the key given to us by the Lord Jesus open the door into the rooms and dimensions of the spirit contained in our inner most beings where we have been made alive and have the kingdom of God within.

We may venture into the limitless expanding realms that have been opened up to us as believers, from there after we have entered into the spirit and used the authority given to us and the commission to rule and reign with Him, we can take what we have been provided and effect the physical world with the Kingdom of God that is within us.

From the outside we have this body as a container, it is frail and made to a limited size and capacity quite mortal, but inside we have our inner man that is made alive by the resurrection power by the Spirit of God and this is where endless possibilities are birthed.

There are many pyramid schemes hatched and operating in this world.

I will just focus on two, there are many more that are similar but these two are like opposites but have a another sinister similarity, in that they are both systems of control that have the multitudes of slaves that serve their system and these are like mysteries as we can't quite put our finger on them and reveal who is operating and what schemes they pull, but we do have by investigation and discernment as well as whistle blowers, under the radar stealth investigators searching out through their frustration and suspicions with determination to expose their atrocities keeping nations in slavery and control.

There are two books which *George Orwell* authored, *Animal Farm* and *1984*.
Animal behaviour, a bit like *Charles Darwin's* *"survival of the fittest,"* the cunning and the manipulators rule over the rest. Animals, is a brilliant allegory where the pigs with a devious greedy nature, see the world as opportunities to move to the top and control, then you have the sheep that go along with the program, trusting and submissive that's just what we need for any plot to run smoothly, just move with the crowd.

As well as the ones that bite back and rebel, but are on a leash and contained and trained like dogs, go on be a rebel we got you.
In the book *1984* is a brilliant depiction of how a State Controlling Government uses its power and means to control the minds and resources of the masses.

Let's call the first Pyramid Scheme an *Orwellian* State Control Dictatorship over the masses, that has its plebs under subjection by tyranny and clever propaganda campaigns using thought shaping technologies that direct their subjects thinking, ensuring that all will conform to the parties wishes, otherwise be hunted down and reprogrammed, or eliminated like a pest, to the wishes of the elitists programming at the top of the pyramid.

Advantages being in the party means accumulated wealth and party privileges while the peasants and workers classes are fed a ration, just enough to survive and remain dependant on the system.

They use big brother surveillance and police state measures to contain the masses under their control.

Just good old outright no questions asked control, very blatant, obvious, if you don't like it we will shoot you.

Pyramid Scheme number two.

Let's say it is a global brave new world, deeper
state cabal elite, big on mind control.
This pyramid is well known, it is displayed on
the bill with its roving eye.

Big Brother is watching you.

They usually operate by stealth and create
puppets to run their duties, who they have
bought out using their great wealth and
corruption and then alter the laws of the land to
allow their policies to run, these policies appear
to be good for all, but are in reality for the
purposes of their agenda.

This system is not up front control, subtle
persuasion coaxing your subjects into the pit
using methods to enslave without people
knowing what's going on, frogs in the boiling pot
slowly turn the heat up type of tricks. You need
to persuade the people to allow it with so called
promise of liberties, but it uses fake liberties to
enslave people with pharmaka, toxic food,
mysterious technologies and entertainment to
corrupt people's minds. Keep the workers who
are struggling to make ends meet amused with
entertainment, make sure they in a haze of
confusion about reality, use media and dark
philosophy to promote the desensitisation to the
corruption of society.

Forget about Mondays, just give me the weekend
make me feel better, forget the stress and the
strain and my aches and pains.

In the minds and imaginations of the
population.
Evil becoming good.
Good becoming evil.
Strange technology beamed all around.
The elite are ruling alright but they are
corrupted.
The spirit of the air has got them; they are
getting orders from a higher power.
No one is free under this system.
The cunning schemes of corrupted twisted
megalomaniacs, hungry for world domination at
any cost, who have connected themselves to the
hive mind, where the AI connected to the cosmic
sciences, downloads in a flash logarithms and
plottings to predict the human race.
They get their directives from the upper levels in
the ether.
They were in the mysterious school, learnt the
trade and can read the ancient symbols.
In the Black Arts summoning up the higher
entities into the host.

Our DNA was good until they messed with it.
Human 2.0 upgrade they tell you, the old
human model is now deleted and any old models
still in circulation will be called in for culling or
conditioning.
A sick society indeed, strange dead strains
programmes that infiltrate the host system
released and infecting the masses.
Doesn't matter we are dumbed down and
oblivious or in a drugged state, meanwhile our
freedoms and rights are violated.

It's in the food, it's in the water, it's in the pills, it's even in the airwaves what channel frequency are you on?

As in the days of Noah.
You've watched those apocalypse state control movies, pure fiction maybe you say.
The machine and AI have taken over, with trans human species on the rise and quite extreme, so many movies have an elite running the ship and the rest are slaves to the system, and you are put into a survival of the fittest scenarios, games to the death, different classes of people, superior races, total breakdowns of society, replaced by the New Order. Brave New World Order or Chaos.

Predictive or prophetic, helps to say I have seen this before and now it is here just like they said, this is better than the movie, wipe out.
Are you a sheep, or a goat, a snarling dog, or a big fat pig living it up in the mud?
Sheep are OK if they follow the right Shepherd and not be devoured by the wolf.

Are either of these Pyramids the Kingdom of God with Jesus as their Lord and Saviour? You decide.
Are they serving another master? There are Agents patrolling the system working for the Master Psycho Architect, they are watching using advanced techno and intrusive surveillance and keeping their evil eye on their subjects, enforcers of the grandiose scheme.

So Christianity is the truth! Better to say Jesus
is the way the truth and the life.

Christianity are the representatives only,
surprise, surprise they are not God, do they
always do what is right given that they are
imperfect beings and can choose what they will
do?
Answer is no.
Look at The Book of Revelation in the Bible.
The letter to the churches.
Jesus meek and mild Shepherd is now the
Glorified King of kings, He is telling off the
churches of the day for corruption and mixed up
beliefs, like serving two masters and He
commends those who overcome.

All had things in common and shared their
resources, looked after the poor. *Acts 2*
Christianity when it is practiced as Christ would
have it is pure.

So don't blame God for Christians messing up,
welcome to the human race, we have all missed
the mark and are going to muck up, but that
doesn't mean God approves of it.
He has a way for us to change our ways, called
repentance, be accepted back on to the track
and be transformed into His likeness. We are a
work in progress, we don't get there until Jesus
returns or the restoration of all things, the
manifestation of the Sons of God.

Why do a small handful of people want to
control the world?

The answer escapes reason.
How do you become a Hitler or Napoleon?

What motivates a person to be a dictator or a hidden wealthy ruling elitist that controls masses by owning the bank or the gold and moving chess pieces around controlling nations' economies, using war, resources, shortages, boom and bust? Maybe even plagues.

What is that? What makes people tick tock that way? A large warped clock out of synch with what is good for others and the planet.
Gets back to the spirit of the world, the god of this world, not the creator, that's God, He doesn't need to control the world, He already owns it, He sent His Son to die for us so we could all be saved. Saved from the system.

So what does the future look like if we take this system to its apex of finality?

Revelation 17
Then one of the seven angels who had the seven bowls came and talked with me, saying to me, "Come, I will show you the judgment of the great harlot who sits on many waters,
2 with whom the kings of the earth committed fornication, and the inhabitants of the earth were made drunk with the wine of her fornication."
3 So he carried me away in the Spirit into the wilderness. And I saw a woman sitting on a scarlet beast which was full of names of blasphemy, having seven heads and ten horns.

4 The woman was arrayed in purple and scarlet, and adorned with gold and precious stones and pearls, having in her hand a golden cup full of abominations and the filthiness of]her fornication.
5 And on her forehead a name was written:
MYSTERY, BABYLON THE GREAT,
THE MOTHER OF HARLOTS AND OF THE
ABOMINATIONS OF THE EARTH.
6 I saw the woman, drunk with the blood of the saints and with the blood of the martyrs of Jesus. And when I saw her, I marveled with great amazement.
7 But the angel said to me, "Why did you marvel? I will tell you the mystery of the woman and of the beast that carries her, which has the seven heads and the ten horns.
8 The beast that you saw was, and is not, and will ascend out of the bottomless pit and go to perdition. And those who dwell on the earth will marvel, whose names are not written in the Book of Life from the foundation of the world, when they see the beast that was, and is not, and yet is.
9 "Here is the mind which has wisdom: The seven heads are seven mountains on which the woman sits.
10 There are also seven kings. Five have fallen, one is, and the other has not yet come. And when he comes, he must continue a short time.
11 The beast that was, and is not, is himself also the eighth, and is of the seven, and is going to perdition.

12 "The ten horns which you saw are ten kings who have received no kingdom as yet, but they receive authority for one hour as kings with the beast.
13 These are of one mind, and they will give their power and authority to the beast.
14 These will make war with the Lamb, and the Lamb will overcome them, for He is Lord of lords and King of kings; and those who are with Him are called, chosen, and faithful."
15 Then he said to me, "The waters which you saw, where the harlot sits, are peoples, multitudes, nations, and tongues.
16 And the ten horns which you saw on the beast, these will hate the harlot, make her desolate and naked, eat her flesh and burn her with fire.
17 For God has put it into their hearts to fulfill His purpose, to be of one mind, and to give their kingdom to the beast, until the words of God are fulfilled.
18 And the woman whom you saw is that great city which reigns over the kings of the earth."
So there are mysteries, things are not as they appear and are hidden until revealed.
We will marvel at their accomplishments, their technologies, their sophistication, their beauty, their dazzle and splendour, but in the end the corruption will dissolve and breakdown into their destruction. You can't play god, be your own god and deny the One True God.

Beginning of sorrows.
Sorrows are like waves that keep coming in greater intensity and frequency as we draw closer to the end of days.

Time and Date is unknown *(10, 20, 30, 50, 100 years?)* but we can know the seasons.
Prophets all over the world, a lot of excellent voices, speaking hearing and seeing from our Fathers perspective.

Yes the days are getting darker, but the light is also getting brighter as believers rise up into their call and authority, God always is ahead of the troubles.
The lockdown will bring some devastating results economically all over, so we will need wisdom to come out stronger in these days.
So, what will see? More cosmic manipulations, electromagnetism alterations, waves like frequencies set into the play into the world stage, configurations, reading into the code of the hive mind machine, the shadows are speaking their devices, we are held in the vices, with techno animated AI robots, got expression from somewhere in the quantum, there is a hope on the horizon, the human race is not forgotten, it won't be left until we are all lizard machine.

There is talk about wars and rumours of wars, plagues, strange signs in the skies as the asteroid approaching, spark and friction tension is high, war of the kingdoms. The scene is set; it is time that we are met: remember 2000 years ago a Saviour was born. On the Clouds of Heaven He comes, so we are not done.
Before it's too late and the show is over and then book is finally closed, you have choice, it's yours and you can use it one way or another!

Steam Engines.
One of the most powerful forces is good old steam.
When a Hot Water Cylinder explodes it is massive.
Revival of the old steam engines.
I love steam trains, the sounds they make, the classic look and character uniqueness, just a good old purity about them, they make me feel youthful and vibrant.

The *Lumsden Heritage Trust*, a local steam train enthusiasts society in New Zealand have recently pulled an old steam train buried in mud for 93 years after being dumped there in the muddy Oreti River.
The enthusiasts are hoping to bring revival to the old classic 1885 V class steam locomotives that were in a sad state, laying waste in the mud for many years.

Are you old and past it, feel like your best years have gone and you have ended up in the muddy pit of societies dumping ground? Well there is Good News on the horizon as old treasures that were considered to be on the rust heap are being revived and restored to reveal all their appreciated character and purpose.

Old treasures with the new that's how we will overcome.

Water is a pure source - sustainable. Rivers of living water is powerful energy within our beings. Although coal was used in the old days.

It is black and sooty and not that great for the atmosphere, there is a lot worse mind you. Now we are getting new energy efficient methods.
Signs and wonders, miracles, Jesus said we will do the greater works.
Greater is He that is in you than he that is in the world.
The same Spirit that raised Jesus from the dead lives in us - revival inside our mortal bodies.
Before Jesus returns will He find faith on the earth?
He will send His Elijah to prepare the way.
Before the end there will be a great end time harvest of souls.
The Gospel will preached to all peoples and nations.

Let's not focus on what the dark agendas are doing, it's all part of the sorrows beginning and intensifying as we draw closer to the end.

We can all do our part right now, if we are old and in the scrap heap rusting to bits, be revived, if we are young, we can learn from the old and experienced and be innovative and design the new ways to conquer.

We can still use the old fuel which is pure water, it still works today.

Make way, get your ticket, get on board, it is a full steam ahead revival coming.

Chapter 4

A Ruse

There is hope for us to see what actually is going on!
So much propaganda, misinformation outright lies, statistics that are biased, twisted like a weaving serpent hypnotising its prey.

Isaiah 32
3 The eyes of those who see will not be dim,
And the ears of those who hear will listen.
4 Also the heart of the rash will understand knowledge,
And the tongue of the stammerers will be ready to speak plainly.
5 The foolish person will no longer be called generous,
Nor the miser said to be bountiful;
6 For the foolish person will speak foolishness,
And his heart will work iniquity:
To practice ungodliness,
To utter error against the LORD,
To keep the hungry unsatisfied,
And he will cause the drink of the thirsty to fail.
7 Also the schemes of the schemer are evil;
He devises wicked plans
To destroy the poor with lying words,
Even when the needy speaks justice.

Are there fools currently who are called generous for supposedly doing good for the well-being of all?

Are the ruling super rich really holding back funds to where it will really make a difference, while donating to a cause which is the agenda? Description of a fool, a worker of iniquity, speaking error and lies, practices ungodly acts. Speaks against the Lord. In other words proud, conceited and an over inflated opinion of self-importance.

They keep the poor hungry and those who have, they take away what little they did have.

They want the working poor middle class.

They disempower people so they can have power over the people.

They pollute the purity in the essential water supply.

Harmful additives.

Schemes, devises wicked plans to destroy mankind, sound familiar? Even when the common man speaks the truth and exposes the lies, he is squashed and silenced.

Matthew 24
42 Watch therefore, for you do not know what hour your Lord is coming.
43 But know this that if the master of the house had known what hour the thief would come, he would have watched and not allowed his house to be broken into.
44 Therefore you also be ready, for the Son of Man is coming at an hour you do not expect.

Your house is your body.

What does it mean to be broken into?

Our cells, our DNA?

Our genome synthetically engineered.

Allowing an abomination into our beings.

Matthew 24
*3 Now as He sat on the Mount of Olives, the
disciples came to Him privately, saying, "Tell us,
when will these things be? And what will be the
sign of Your coming, and of the end of the age?"
4 And Jesus answered and said to them: "Take
heed that no one deceives you.
5 For many will come in My name, saying, 'I am
the Christ,' and will deceive many.
6 And you will hear of wars and rumours of wars.
See that you are not troubled; for all these things
must come to pass, but the end is not yet.
7 For nation will rise against nation, and kingdom
against kingdom. And there will be famines,
pestilences, and earthquakes in various places.
8 All these are the beginning of sorrows.*

Some signs to watch out for.
Matthew 24
*12 And because lawlessness will abound, the love
of many will grow cold.
13 But he who endures to the end shall be saved.
14 And this gospel of the kingdom will be
preached in all the world as a witness to all the
nations, and then the end will come.*

No one knows.
Matthew 24
*36 "But of that day and hour no one knows, not
even the angels of heaven, but My Father only.
37 But as the days of Noah were, so also will the
coming of the Son of Man be.*

So What is the Origin of the Virus?
Answer.

The origin of the virus is Satanic!
This means those who are involved with it are tools of Satan.
Satan's fools what are you playing at?
You don't want to be involved in that.
It is a curse, it has power and you might feel like Dr Frankenstein, *"I am a science god, I am playing god, look I can destroy mankind what power."*
But in the end it is from the pit of hell, entering through the gates of hell.

Yes God may use what was intended for evil to be turned around and we may need to be adjusted, tuned in, examine our hearts to see if there be any anxiety in us that offends.

Nations in the balance, Kingdoms shaken, displacements like tectonic plates being realigned.
The knowledge of the Glory of God will fill the earth.

Do you see the ruse in play?
The definition of a ruse may help you to see what is really going on here!

A Ruse is a planned trick with the intention to deceive people and it has been well orchestrated to conceal the true intentions of the instigator.

Here is a riddle that would make The Riddler proud. *Batman and Batwoman.*

Unique inserts spike pattern, gain of function Sars Mers Corona cocktail mix, a gain of entry host hack, with retro viruses lurking our immune response is on fire! Who is responsible or is something behind the Who? Bats soup stirred in the lab going viral onto the world, they patented it, they published it, peer reviewed it, still alluded it, the scientific godfathers knew what was in the brew, locked up society composed a solution, inserted and tattooed tracking the DNA infused, the drones are watching all, temperatures are rising, don't worry we got masks and not shaking the hands anymore, antibodies anti our body deadly strain the brain, you got this figured out where it came from?

Here is what the Prophet of the Lord is seeing.

Habakkuk 2
Then the Lord answered me and said:
"Write the vision
And make it plain on tablets,
That he may run who reads it.
3 For the vision is yet for an appointed time;
But at the end it will speak, and it will not lie.
Though it tarries, wait for it;
Because it will surely come,
It will not tarry.
4 "Behold the proud,
His soul is not upright in him;
But the just shall live by his faith.

This is the assurance, what is already established will come to pass no matter what things look like in the natural, there is an appointed time for everything.

Habakkuk 2
5 "Indeed, because he transgresses by wine,
He is a proud man,
And he does not stay at home.
Because he enlarges his desire as hell,
And he is like death, and cannot be satisfied,
He gathers to himself all nations
And heaps up for himself all peoples.
6 "Will not all these take up a proverb against him,
And a taunting riddle against him, and say,
'Woe to him who increases
What is not his—how long?
And to him who loads himself with many pledges'?
7 Will not your creditors rise up suddenly?
Will they not awaken who oppress you?
And you will become their booty.
8 Because you have plundered many nations,
All the remnant of the people shall plunder you,
Because of men's blood
And the violence of the land and the city,
And of all who dwell in it.
9 "Woe to him who covets evil gain for his house,
That he may set his nest on high,
That he may be delivered from the power of disaster!
10 You give shameful counsel to your house,
Cutting off many peoples,
And sin against your soul.

11 For the stone will cry out from the wall,
And the beam from the timbers will answer it.
12 "Woe to him who builds a town with
bloodshed,
Who establishes a city by iniquity!
13 Behold, is it not of the Lord of hosts
That the peoples labour to feed the fire,
And nations weary themselves in vain?
14 For the earth will be filled
With the knowledge of the glory of the Lord,
As the waters cover the sea.

God is bigger than the might of any nation, whether they have the biggest Nukes and the biggest army in the world, ships and planes posted everywhere menacing the waters.

Whether they are the scheming cunning hidden players in cahoots, manipulating all of the economies of the world, playing chess and mind warping games with the masses who are the pawns in this epic battle.

Gods Kingdom is the most powerful of any force in all of creation and it is far above any kingdom of this earth, the bible says the Nations Rage against the righteous, but they are fools, the bible also says that God looks down upon the nations that appear to be like ants and drops in the ocean, they are in reality a small, weak puny mortal thing. Do not provoke the Lord you fools, that is not wise.

Arrogance and foolishness will rage for a time,
but in the eternal seasons that is like just a
moment that will pass and fade away to nothing.
We pray your Kingdom come and your will be
done on earth as it is in Heaven.
There are no goat nations in heaven, so these
are not His will on earth.
All nations can change their ways and turn
around and surrender their future to the Lord.
That is what believers can do, when we have
repented from our foolish ways and returned to
the Lord, we can then pray according to His will
and the mountains of impossibilities will move
from their position of pride and violence and be
thrown into the sea.

Time will play out and then suddenly like a
tsunami it will make its impact with force and
remove all who resist in its path.

Good News for those who are believers in Jesus
our Lord and Saviour, He is the way the truth
and the life.
We are delivered from the bondage of corruption
into His Glory and Liberty as Sons of God,
Rom 8.
We rule and reign.
Walk on top of the waves - walk above by faith
the fire storms afflicting like a plague.

Not by might.
Not by Power.
But by My Spirit says the Lord.
The Mountain is removed. *Zechariah*

What mountain? The mountain opposed to the true unadulterated Temple of God which houses the Kingdom within. The mountain that is like a Ziggurat and a Towering Babel, a regime that pollutes the body and the souls of men, subject to their master with the roving eye, ruling principalities captured the minds and blinded them to the truth, whether be by force or free will they are deceived by a strong delusion.

Rise up like Sons and Daughters of the Most High, Pray, Decree and Declare as directed; your faith will move mountains as He promised, greater works you will do.

This is our promise.
Isaiah 32
17 And the work of righteousness shall be peace; and the effect of righteousness quietness and assurance for ever.
18 And my people shall dwell in a peaceable habitation, and in sure dwellings, and in quiet resting places;

Do you want to be a slave of the system or free? Remember it is because of Him that we are made righteous; this is not of ourselves so that no man can boast.

The blood of Jesus cleanses us from all of the effects of sin, there is life in the blood. When we are contaminated, He cleanses us makes us whole again, we have the DNA of God, made in His image, not in a test tube by a mad scientist from the Brave New World Order.

We have His assurance that it is a done deal.
Assurance is better than false security.

The just will live by his faith.

Chapter 5

Woke up Call

The John 17 solution.
The Body of Christ is One in Christ Jesus.
All in one accord, all of the same mind, we can all have the correct way of thinking with the Mind of Christ and work things out together.

If you are not yet in Christ, well OK in the coming days when the Glory of God fills this rough old earth, you will want to get on board, because honestly this is the only solution to all of the worlds troubles which are escalating out of control in 2020. Trouble between nations, trouble on the borders, trouble with the police on the streets, trouble between Government parties, nuclear troubles and threats, trouble with race and now violence in our communities, not just any old riot.
You might be able to see the hidden causes.
You might be able to hear what the people are saying.
You might be feeling the pain.
Smell trouble.
Tasting something off.
When we are walking, the left and the right move together with balanced feet.
Two hands can work together to build.
You don't want your own hand fighting against you, you would slap it!
Your right hand builds then your left hand pulls it down.

What the!
I can't handle this anymore says the left hand
and pulls it down.
The right hand says I am the dominate one, the
favoured and stronger hand, that's just how it is,
but then you have a left handed person so there
you go, there is the other side of power.

What I am trying to say, we need each other in
our diversities to make the whole thing work out
better.
The body is diverse, like many races, gifts and
ways of thinking, like different perspectives to
make it a complete picture.
Diversity is a good thing.
The body works together as a unit for the
common good, the body needs all of its members
to function, holistically.

The Manifold wisdom of God is expressed
through His diverse members of the Body of
Christ on earth.
Ephesians 3
*[10] to the intent that now the manifold wisdom of
God might be made known by the church to the
principalities and powers in the heavenly places,*
Let's be working it all out together and moving
together to build a better world.
This is what St Paul wrote about 2000 years ago.
Let's not pull him down.

The world is staged.
Just saying, this is just what I am seeing right
now!
Getting justice doesn't equal lawlessness.

There is an old saying two wrongs don't make a right.
You don't call black white do you, that's just how it is!

As for the ones who are going out protesting, good on you, go with your cause and get your voice heard, there were protests in the 1960s, it was all about love and peace and equality, I am all for that.
But now I am hearing dismantle the police force because of some rotten apples in the bunch.
Ok yes we could work towards reforms that's fine, let's improve, upgrade, educate, remove bad cultures.

The world isn't perfect so let's work together to make it a better place, all hands on deck, collaboration, cooperation, the police are here to serve the community and uphold the law to protect us against violence to persons and property.

As for those who have a legitimate cause, I hear you, I can see that there is real pain. Society isn't perfect and hopefully we as a people aim to be progressively learning from the errors of the past and building constructively towards a better future for everyone.
We won't build a better world by wrecking the joint, who is going to respect that? From both sides, we all need to get together, sit down and listen and think about how to answer with respect of other party, not running each other down.

Now if someone is wrecking your place then
there would be words for sure and you should
take action to defend.
Looting, destroying, pulling down, dismantling
by violence, that is not how we progressively
negotiate.

Don't get mad I am just saying what is right and
should be the done thing!
You've seen the kid throwing a tantrum when
they don't get their own way, what do you say
"hey hey hey that's not OK".

I am saying we need to wake up, move on and
advance in this 21st century, do things in a new
way, yes reforms if necessary, talk it through,
allow time for the system to be upgraded and
retrained, let's get a grip, things don't need to be
messed up!

In this wonderful democratic government, we
have been given a right to protest and voice our
concerns to alert the authorities that there is
something wrong with our moral compass and a
correction is required, justice should be
something that brave people go after and follow
through to see change.

Things that cause cancers in our societies
should be demonstrated against for sure.
However, this is done within the rules of society,
peaceably without violence, best not to correct a
wrong in society by committing wrongs on that
society.

When Jesus walked the earth He was full of compassion and was motivated by love and He stood for what was right and justice for all. Jesus wept, He felt our pain, He wept as He knew that there is a lot of needless suffering and

He saw how far we have fallen from the original plan and the place of perfect peace and harmony in the garden of Eden before we were sold a lie, I am relating us all to Adam and Eve as they believed the lie of Satan, that we could all be gods and make our own laws of right and wrong and here you have it in our world today, making our own laws, living our own ways based on our own ways of judging one another and how we relate to others who don't agree with how we believe things should be, because we know better than God, so we believe the lie, we are wise in our own eyes, think we are better than the others and treat them accordingly, totally self-important and full of ourselves.

What I am seeing these days on the world stage with many actors looking to make a name for themselves, make their smear on society, 5 minutes of fame on YouTube, increasing violence under the cover of a cause, throwing bricks through the windows, looting and destruction on someone else's property, fires burning on someone else's property, antaganegotistic mayhem, livelihoods and people's lives threatened, but no don't let it be threats on your own life as you are a hero!

The paramilitary is uprising, they are coming out in the cover of the dark night, they are driven by dangerous subversive ideologies.
The stinking think-tank elite need brainwashed henchmen to do their dirty work, while they sit smug behind the scenes, tucked away in fortified super rich mansions, far removed from what they have unleashed on the regular people, violence that they wouldn't tolerate on their own doorstep, they resist the laws, attack the law officers upholding it, they are OK with funding the violence, yet they say the police should be defunded when they are trying to stop violence, this all started by the unhealed history of pain and violence so why try to fix it with violence?

Remember the law enforcement don't hold the sword for nothing. Hatred increasing between different parties, the great divide who will conquer, stirring up racial wars, now nations are disputing borders all the way into the oceans; are we in perilous times?
The Song by the Beatles called Revolution has some relevant lyrics about fixing the world, we all might be idealists, but we don't go about it by destroying and destruction, that is not OK! John Lennon a revolutionary is saying, wake up there is a better way to help the world than mindless maniacs destroying everything.

There is one word that fits what I see - lawlessness!
Trying to change the laws of God and the times and seasons, wear down what is good and proper.

What is the real fight about?

Is the war on another hidden level, principalities and rulers of darkness inciting those to do their cruel masters bidding?

Defying absolutes, they say there is no black or white, yet there is a race issue about black and white.

They don't really care about race and riots, cull the worlds population by any means including any race, religion, party, nation, pit them against each other, sit back and watch the violence unfold, they really just want to use whatever fuel they can find, using it for their own agenda of violence and hatred.

I am just saying what if a mob of certain professional agitators turned up at a certain financers home and demanded higher pay for high risk employment, possible arrest, prison sentence, violent reaction from angry shop owners whose store got trashed, chanting *"more pay George more pay."* How would this be met? An army of militia security I suppose.

Let's look closer at popular philosophies that do not abide by the universal laws of right and wrong which are absolutes.

Situational ethics, what is right for one is not right in another situation, this is meant to result in fairness for all and peace, not destruction or abuse of others.

There is a black and there is a white, don't you agree, so we have like two different states? Black and White, like Good and Evil, right and left, right and wrong, what are these absolutes.

Yet we have their argument, two wrongs make a right.
In shifting ethics it depends on the situation what makes it right, but even this opposing view to absolutes would not accept two wrongs make a right. Situational ethics is meant to point to a higher way above the current laws.

Psychologists aim to modify our behaviour by using positive stimuli and *Kohlberg has developed six stages of moral development* which aims to move us towards an ideal morality. Are you those with moral fibre who would not approve of psychologists that propose, achieving a better society using high voltage shock treatment and violence against others? Psycho destruction is going down the slippery slope of evil behaviour!

I don't see these principles of ethical development applied with what I am witnessing today, thugs let loose with no restraints.

The Song by the Beatles called Revolution has some more relevant lyrics about getting money from people who want to destroy others to fulfil their agenda of hate. They are idealists who use their resources to bring harm and destruction to our world, paying the mob to carry out their evil plans against others.

Tell me please instigators what are you creating and where is this headed, even if you remove the current governments and administrations, the violence won't stop they will continue against what is the left, because there will always be a cause and effect if you tried to make two wrongs a right, you have released the destroyer who is bent on destruction even in your own brave new utopia they will still be hell-bent, because two wrongs don't make a right? Wrong is not Right no matter how you spin it.

The Song by the Beatles called Revolution has even more relevant lyrics about freeing your mind. Chairman Mao and regimes that follow similar practices impose extremist measures on society, destroying others in the process. Especially, those who are not sitting dummies and oppose the atrocity of loss of freedoms that are our basic human rights! Psycho Captains doing evil stuff to others won't fix anything. In other words in your ideologist blindness, don't be evil as well with your selfish ambitions to change the world.

Let me contrast what the world needs now is Good News. God is love, if we all surrender our past pains and hurts and are healed by Jesus we will take on His nature, we have the character of love in our hearts towards our fellow man whether we agree with them or not. Don't be our own law unto ourselves, imposing what we think is the right thing to do on others usually to harm them.

God also operates with justice, He does not tolerate violence and hatred and will demand justice for the oppressed and the abused.

Compassion for the oppressed, not the oppressor, that's why the law is there for those who do evil to others.

The authorities are there for a reason as long as they abide by Gods laws as they are there to protect and serve and use force if required to stop crimes being committed.

2 Timothy 3 King James Version (KJV)
This know also, that in the last days perilous times shall come.
2 For men shall be lovers of their own selves, covetous, boasters, proud, blasphemers, disobedient to parents, unthankful, unholy,
3 Without natural affection, trucebreakers, false accusers, incontinent, fierce, despisers of those that are good,
4 Traitors, heady, high-minded, lovers of pleasures more than lovers of God;
5 Having a form of godliness, but denying the power thereof: from such turn away.

The Ten Commandments are summed up by Jesus with 2 commandments of Love.
Love God.
Love your neighbour.
This is the highest law and all the laws should have these as their foundation.
If you love God you will also love your brother and your sister.
All are one in God, doesn't matter if you are black or white, yellow or red or brown, we are loved equally and the greater one is the one who serves.
We are all one in Him.

You can't be on the other side of the fence in Him, there is no conservative, no neo liberal sides in Him, no this clan versus that clan, this way or that way inclined, we are all one in Him, brothers and sisters in the Lord and in His ways which are higher than our ways.

No racism there, love is greater. Matter of fact all of our DNA can be traced back to original parents, so way back then we were all in one family.

Yet God wants us to celebrate our diversities, as He is diverse, so it is OK to be different, we are not all carbon copies and dress in the same uniform and talk and think the same way, boring, so celebrate diversity and differences don't make it into a race war that is not God's way of relating to others.

Let me relate a story, when a cyclone hit New Zealand in the late 1990s, *(southern hemisphere version of hurricanes, typhoons, major storm system with high winds).*

I was living in Te Aroha *(which means the mountain of love in Maori)* at this time, had a house there which needed restoration and created a fence made from off cuts from the local saw mill. It was attached to posts concreted in the ground and had a homemade gate made for it. During the night when the storm was at its fiercest, I looked out the side window to see the fence been thrown backwards and forwards, tilting back and forth on its posts in the ground by the intense wind, it was reduced to a tilting, tottering fence flapping around; then to my horror to make matters much worse, what followed this alarming sight of devastation; the unruly wind then proceeded to rip the gate right off and flung it back into the yard. The homemade fence had heaps of character and looked fit for purpose, but it was no match for this intense storm.

Well let me just relate this story to what I am sensing here; at this moment in 2020, it is like a constant barrage of storms and vicious winds just throwing everything about, a hell of a shaking, the gate that kept the wolf out has been ripped off and he has got in roaming around looking to devour, the foundations are weakened and we all need to be rebuilt to withstand the onslaught, but like Te Aroha meaning mountain of love, this is the right place to be, so hang in there, remain in love, rebuild and stand firm, strengthen what remains, put the armour on, defend from anything that would knock the gate off, allowing the enemy access into our nations, cities, communities, lives, to wreak havoc.

Be aware of the possibility of attacks coming right there in your street, remain in Him, don't be distracted or asleep as the enemy wants to rip it all to bits.

When the enemy comes in with his division and waves of inciting hatred, then the Lord will set a tsunami against him to flush him out of the land.

Our part, prayer and then applying our gift whatever we are given to make a difference, learn the lessons from yesterday, be wiser, remain in Him and be part of the solution, not part of the problem, then make the world a better place with our brothers and sisters, together we are better.

Here is Revolution in truth and change for the better.
In the great revivals of the past, starting in the Book of Acts all the way to the Welsh Revival, the Hebrides in Scotland, the English Reformers and of cause the good old USA and many more, whole districts were swept by the Glory of God, people everywhere repented and turned from their wicked ways and as a result crime was virtually non-existent, police had little to do. Doors were not locked at night, people all over helped each other out, looked after the poor and the street people.
It all started with some prayer warriors who did not give up, but tarried until God and His Glory came and revival fires came and lit up peoples broken down lives, spreading all around like a revolution, better said a revival bringing change to the whole of society from the ones at the top in power all the way to the disenfranchised ones with nothing.

Why not start praying for change and let God do the work through His radically saved people and change our communities into places of peace and prosperity with no hatred, no oppression and division wrecking the place.

Rioters, looters, wreckers and angry violent people, you don't have to stay that way, Jesus came to save all, just repent let Him do the rest. Healing will also be the norm, the plague and viruses are no match either for the power of God.

We've all got a part to play, different gifts, different strengths, different ways are all part of the overall solution.

It aint just some smart words that I am saying, that won't change a thing, if we don't have His light then no love, so no matter what we say it just won't really change a thing at all.
If we abide in Him, we are something and agents of change for the better. If we don't have Him in our hearts then we are nothing, void and empty sounding off with dark energy, like a puff of smoke, to be blown away.

We all need to give an account for our actions done.
Gods plan is that the Glory of God will fill the earth and sweep all the violence away by His brightness and love, you will either accept the truth see the error of your ways, worship the King or you will have to run and hide in a dark hole somewhere and stew in your hatred.

Do the golden law, which is do unto others as you would have them do to you.

Peace Out.

The world might be staged, spinning into destruction, but God has a solution for our revolutions.

Are you woken up yet?
Make way, get your ticket, get on board, it is a full steam ahead revival coming.

Chapter 6

We need to fortify the walls of Jerusalem.
That is our Holy City and if the walls are broken
down the undesirable hostiles are getting in to
destroy what we value and ruin the glorious
buildings, our peace will be under threat, society
crumbles and the temple is defiled.
King David wrote Psalm 51 after he committed
adultery and had a person killed to cover his
crime.
David repented of his ways and in conclusion he
said in *Psalm 51*
"Fortify the walls of Jerusalem!" The NET Version
or other versions say *"rebuild the walls of
Jerusalem"*.
The Message is rebuild the ruins and become
strong, secure and offer protection.
Government is about making sure that there are
laws in place and the foundations are in order as
well as upholding the principles of the land.
You need the right people in charge otherwise
the walls come down and there will be
devastation. Society suffers and the people in
the land also suffer defeat.
Romans 1
*21 Because that, when they knew God, they
glorified him not as God, neither were thankful;
but became vain in their imaginations, and their
foolish heart was darkened.*
*22 Professing themselves to be wise, they became
fools,*

"Warning, Warning, Danger, Danger, Will Robinson". Robot from Lost in Space Quote.
Don't put Dr Smith in charge!
Sabotaging the mission, having own agenda, destruction of the mission.
We need a John Robinson in charge, who has got his wits, has values and is about protecting the family unit and staying on the course, immovable. Then maybe a Major West to navigate and ensure that the controls are working.
Professor Robinson requires justice and he will not allow evil aliens entering the perimeter to bring destruction on lives and property.
Characters from Lost in Space TV Show and Movies.

The good.
The bad.
And the Ugly. *From Title of Movie.*

We are all in a shoot-out figuratively speaking.
There is the drawing of guns and facing off for battle.
What can we do in these times and who can save us?
Pray and more prayer.

1 Timothy 2
Therefore I exhort first of all that supplications, prayers, intercessions, and giving of thanks be made for all men,
2 for kings and all who are in authority, that we may lead a quiet and peaceable life in all godliness and reverence.

3 For this is good and acceptable in the sight of God our Saviour,
4 who desires all men to be saved and to come to the knowledge of the truth.
5 For there is one God and one Mediator between God and men, the Man Christ Jesus,
6 who gave Himself a ransom for all, to be testified in due time,
Do we see peace and godliness?
Pray and more prayer.

Are Schools and Institutions teaching students and young children how to think or what to think?
What do you think?
So the answer is comply or else, fill in the blanks with what they tell you and you will pass.
Is that critical thinking?

Romans 1
25 Who changed the truth of God into a lie, and worshipped and served the creature more than the Creator, who is blessed for ever. Amen.

Yin and Yen the flower pot men.
Tweedle Dee and Tweedle Dum.
We sound the same, but in realty not the same, are we mixed up?

Free to speak, individuals?
Political Correctness, Monitoring Ministry of Thought Police.
Darkness is absorbing all of the light so you can't see what is real.
Delusions abound.

Light reflects all colours so you can see and appreciate the truth.

Colours are amazing variations, nuances, so we are constantly enlightened.

Wisdom doesn't make us conform to the pattern of this world, which is being controlled by dark agendas and totalitarian rulers imposing corrupted ideologies.
Unity governed by peace is good as this does not lead to violence and destruction.

If we have the Mind of Christ, our thoughts are from a trusted source.
We can work it out when there are differences and the colours aren't the same.

He translated us out of the Kingdom of Darkness into His Glorious Kingdom of Light.

When in darkness you stumble around, not knowing where you are going and where you will end up, you can't see the true face of those who are calling the shots leading the mob into the pit.

What we need is a challenge.

This is the challenge called M.

The Riddler is back, Batman and Batwoman.
Characters from Batman TV Show and Movies.

Can you find the clues in M?

M
Muse Me M
Modifications Mayhem Messing Munity
Manipulation Mouse Mutations Medications
Malignant Models Murder Mystery Mortality
Mint More Money Missing Millions
Making Monitored Masses Misery
Malicious Managing Mad Men
Mafia Militia Mercenaries Mobsters
Mayhem Mounted Madness
Megalomaniac Mismanaged Municipalities
Mirrored Maligned Messed Movements
Most Modernism Morons Maulings
Matter Mutter Mental Minions Marauders
Missing Mark Masked Monster
Mocking Minds Manipulating Masses Media
Meddling Mentioned Material
Minced Measured Mixed Messages
Missing Messing Muzzling
Mad Mad Mad Master Movie
Monumental Marxism Morose Mao
More Musing Mr Murky Mule
Me Move Mission Manage Miracle
Magnificent Mighty Moses
Enough of the M.

Just as well there is Good News
Romans 1
*[16] For I am not ashamed of the gospel of Christ,
for it is the power of God to salvation for everyone
who believes, for the Jew first and also for the
Greek.*
*[17] For in it the righteousness of God is revealed
from faith to faith; as it is written,
"The just shall live by faith."*

This is Revolution.
Rewrite our Future.
With the Good News.
The Gospel.
This is the Power of God to save us.
Redeem our Past.
Rewritten into our Now.
This is our Future.

We are One with Him seated in the Heavenly
Realms which is above any ruling class on earth.

Be Blessed.
Peace.

Chapter 7

Conspiracy Construct Composite

Why have the sinister forces constructed a
Firewall? For the purpose of blocking the truth
from being freely published, exchanging the
truth with lies which enables their agenda only
to be heard, on top of this the thought and
speech control police attack voices who oppose
their ideology and if possible disappear these
soldiers of truth and any whistle-blowers.

This refers to worldwide Quantum AI blockchain
entanglements, not just one or more related
obvious countries, the rest just learn from all of
their tricks and introduce it incrementally!!!

Is Capitalism the real enemy?
Why oppose wealth creation?

Families, trades people, skilled workers,
professionals and businesses these are the
backbone that support our Nation.
Keeping people in jobs, supplying for the family,
providing a future for the children.

Putting money back into the community when
buying supplies and products as well as living
essentials, this makes the economy tick over and
provides health for the community.

Wealth circulates and should be a benefit for all
who partake in supporting this system.

If you are a university student you study get a qualification then when you graduate you need to find employment, when lots of graduates are leaving university they need a healthy economy to supply jobs and continue the cycle, of input and output, giving and receiving.

Keep planting good seeds, not modified seeds that don't reproduce.

Farmers sow seeds and produce fruitful supplies, which is the food for the nation, we learn from the sowing and reaping principle. As well as putting something into the community, receiving wages or fruit for your labours adds to the equation, also there is nothing wrong with working smarter to create and generate more wealth for productivity.

Undermining and opposing small business in our communities will destroy the futures of the upcoming generations and create lack and poverty for families who need income to survive; in a healthy flowing economy these will produce overflow to feed back into the economy creating a circulation of supply. When you take away something or destroy something good and productive, you have a minus, minuses in this context are negative and are not good for anyone.

Building houses provides work for builders and the construction industry workers, buying products locally or manufactured in your country will provide work and incomes for manufacturers and their employees, this is healthy economics.

Don't pull something that is working down and burn it, instead by all means make improvements, restore, be efficient, protect the environment and health of the occupants, upgrade, build a better future.

Change is good and works well as people see the benefits and incorporate the new and exchange it for the old ways in an operation that sees increase, a plus.

The other side of the coin, if you mean capitalism stands for Billionaires who are like the 1% that own about 99%, here we do have a problem. Why! As these, maybe not all, have an agenda that is about domination and elimination of small business owners who can't compete and are paying excessive costs to survive, put under pressure by the mega rich who are obsessed with total control of the masses.

They want to tattoo an ID on everyone and have all under a surveillance system for mass control. Watch out who are you working for when you go out on your mission to destroy?
The working man and the business owners who are contributors to society are not the enemy, they are the health of the nation.

Pawns on the chest board.
Chess Men pawns are the expendable.
While the King Rat is hidden, protected and Queen Jezebel wields great power to remove other chess pieces and manoeuvres around the board, plotting and scheming destruction.

Another observation.

Victorians are prisoners now in a Penal Colony.
I guess that is how Australia was established, an exiled bunch of convicts, separated from Mother Ship England to a colonial island controlled by law enforcement.

Something else that should be observed, notice that there is a C right in the middle of this abbreviation, HCQ? In the middle of this virus, can it be minimised eliminated or isolated? Yes!!! Don't take my word for it, ask an expert who was right there in the thick of it!

According to the expert virologist from Hong Kong Top Lab, *Dr. Li Meng Yan* believes it would work and all of the top brass in many nations know and are taking it, taken following the proper advice, prevention mainly not when you are in hospital on a ventilator.

Disclaimer, I am not an expert or have medical training, follow your own due diligence. Look around there are a lot of experts, doctors, peer reviewed reports recommending it.

The role of Government is to administer and enforce the law, to ensure justice and equity is upheld in the land.

There you have it, this is a right perspective of what the left and the right should be, on the one hand we deliver justice and on the other hand we ensure that it is fair for all.

Equity and Justice, left and right.

This is just how it is, God has established laws, we apply them and create a legal system based on these and it is just and fair, we can rule with the wisdom of Solomon, wisdom from above is peaceable and pure, wisdom from below creates confusion and selfish ambitions.

Government on its own is not our Saviour, but Government run on sound principles brings joy to the people of the land, Government run by fools who oppose sound advice brings corruption, misery and poverty to a nation.

Make a wise choice and things will turn out well for your land.

Observation from history, the left say they are looking after the working people, they promise a utopia and equality for all, but end up creating more unemployment, more dependency on the welfare system, lowering the living standards for families and the working class, elimination of the middle class and struggling businesses with excessive taxes and penalties, but they never touch the elite class who are the mega rich that are running the show and are the ones calling the shots hidden in the slippery shadows.

On the other hand, when we have the shifty Neo Liberalists from the right in charge, then we have a globalist agenda that crushes the profits of businesses who can't compete against slave overseas labour, excessive taxes and penalties, they then get taken over by huge multinational globalist companies; the regular worker can't find jobs due to excessive and non-selective free for all open borders, (nothing wrong with immigration and helping those genuine cases, just not at the expense and detriment of the citizens, especially if what comes in causes destruction in the neighbourhoods). Usually these type of right wingers promise the conservatives that they will uphold proper values and will make changes, but they lie and never do.

Which do you prefer, Neo Liberal takeovers or Leftist Marxist oppression?
Extreme Right and Extreme Left basically operate the same way, exclusion and elimination and control until all must conform to the parties thinking.
Antichrist means an influencing mind control that is opposite to Gods Values.

Conforming to the pattern of this world.
Romans 12
Remember the effects of the firewall masking the truth and creation of the propaganda to influence our minds.

Just checked the time, it says 3:33pm, what does that mean, the truth will set you free.

There is a better choice, can you see it?
God's ways are higher than our ways.
There is a right hand and then there is a left hand both have their place and purpose and work together to build the whole.

Equity, now an abused and stolen buzzword meaning fair for all and Justice make up how things should go.
The correct meaning of these words Equity and Justice is the balanced version of left and right.

However, it isn't necessarily about this party or that side, it is more about values.
Those who support the family and Godliness, encourage businesses to be self-sufficient and profitable contributors to the economy, not those who support global domination takeover powers and introduce overwhelming unreasonable profit sucking policies. We need encouragement of individualism, uniqueness and incentive to achieve, not uniformity in the same drab uniforms or the same mob appearance and mindless clamour, contained on the same limited, dumbed down level, while the elite run the whole thing and enjoy the perks.

Guerrillas are hijacking demonstrations and using people as shields to carry out violence and destruction driven by misguided warped ideologies modelled on big brother and history tells us that millions lost their lives to cruel oppressive totalitarian regimes with no regard for human life, the only thing that matters is their own narcissist selfish ambitions.

OK then! We need some levity, a game, since the powers are playing games with us.

Another puzzling message from the Riddler, Batman and Batwoman, work it out!

Conspiracy Construct Composite
Covert contemptible culpable coalition conglomerates
Cagey camouflaged commie chumps caboodle
Crippling crooked cowards cacophony
Cunning conniving creepy constant cursed coots
Conforming convoluted criminals calamity
Caustic chronic clamour catastrophe
Causes collared convicts colony
Come clear converted

This is the thing, Gods perfect nature demands justice and He hates all rebellion and won't tolerate it, rebellion won't stand in His glorious presence, it will be cast out shrinking away in fear and pathetic slithering away. However, we have all fallen short of Gods perfect ways, we are all goons acting out in rebellion until we come to repentance, turn from our foolish ways and accept His grace and mercy.

I am in no position to judge anyone as we are all sinners and need to repent, I am just a voice reporting what I see and turning the light on, so you can see the whole picture.

There is Good News for all, God is Love and wants no one to perish.

Mercy triumphs over judgement that is Gods will, that none is lost and all would come back to Him as their Heavenly Father who loves us with an eternal love.

It doesn't matter which side you are on, yes being destructive is not good for anyone, as long as you make the right choice and get free of your conformity to the perverted thinking of this world and receive His love and mercy the better it is for all.

Something else to consider is that we are deceived and living in a strong delusion when we are under the pattern of this world and its warped ideologies, there are unseen powers over mankind controlling us like puppets, we are sucked in by their cunning devices to believe lies and act out their sick hateful plans to see mankind destroyed.

The answer for the increasing darkness and destruction happening all across the globe is to step into the light, walk in the light, be in the light as He is in the light, Jesus is the light of mankind and without Him we are stumbling around in darkness making fools of ourselves in the eternal picture.

Turn your eyes upon Jesus
Look full in His wonderful face
And the things of earth will grow strangely dim
In the light of His glory and grace

"Turn Your Eyes Upon Jesus" is a hymn by *Helen Howarth Lemmel* which was inspired by a tract entitled *Focused*, written by the missionary *Isabella Lilias Trotter*.

Remember Elijah's servant.
Open my eyes Lord.
There are more for us than against us.
We have an array of warrior angels on our side.
Psalms 40
6 Sacrifice and offering You did not desire;
My ears You have opened.
Burnt offering and sin offering You did not require.
7 Then I said, "Behold, I come;
In the scroll of the book it is written of me.
8 I delight to do Your will, O my God,
And Your law is within my heart."

The key of being is in the heart of the matter.
Not just following a set of laws.
In your book written in Heaven is the perfect plan for your life, if we walk in the light of this we will find love, joy and peace, we will have fulfilment on earth as it is in Heaven.

From the heart the mouth speaks.
It is about being with your whole being.

We as believers with delegated Authority need to employ the angels.

Pray and seek the Lord for wisdom, strategies, and your part in His army.

Be bold and rise up in the strength of a ruling and reigning, roaring lion, establish justice and righteousness, let the people in the land rejoice for what the Lord has done, marvellous things, miracles as He has routed the enemies of the land.

Declare what you have been given from Heaven and shift the darkness on earth to be as He says it is. Amen.

Chapter 8

Seeing beyond 2020 Vision

I can see black and I can see white.
I can see the darkness and I can see the light.
I can see that there is the night and now I can
see the daylight arising.

Kingdom of Darkness.
Kingdom of Light.
Gain of Function DNA Altering Invasion.
There is a lot of shenanigans going on!
The Glory of God will fill the earth and displace
the darkness.
Calling for the Transformation of Sons and
Daughters of God Manifested.

Seeing beyond 2020 Vision

For every negative force there is a reaction by an
equal and opposite positive force, naturally
works as in *Newton's Law*.
However The Law of the Spirit of Life has a
different outcome!

This law supernaturally works over and above
and also works as a higher level law in the
natural.

Greater is He that is in us than he that is in the
world.

Satan was expelled from Heaven, he fell like lightning, the Kingdom of Light rules and reigns, believers have been given all authority over the power of Satan and his leagues of devils.
We have resurrection power, we are having a supernatural experience on top of a limited natural dimension on earth.

Therefore this supernatural law is interpreted as every negative force is met by an overwhelming far superior positive force that destroys the work of the negative force and eliminates its effect, sends it packing back into the black hole it came from.
It also can be redescribed this way, a force of the kingdom of darkness is met by the greater force from the Kingdom of Light which will obliterate it to kingdom come.

Only believe, take a hold of it, apply it, pray into it, align with it, and follow His lead.
When you apply faith into the natural realm, its properties are altered down to the sub atomic levels which changes our very DNA.

Seeing beyond means given insight beyond what is visible and perceived in the natural.
It is when you are given sight from above to see things like God sees things that takes us there, where all things are possible.
When you have 2020 vision that is as good as it gets in the natural, however God takes us beyond the boundaries and He enables us to see beyond the natural, then we are seeing into the all things are possible realms.

They say quantum physics opens up all sorts of possibilities.
Well faith is the substance of things hoped for. What do we see in the natural happening right now in the world? A lot of disruption, a menacing virus creating economic woes, society in lockdown imprisoned by fear and control, confusion over what is the truth. There is the racial conflicts making a storm, wars between different factions, ideologies warping into riots and destruction of what is proper, speech police, AI algorithms cancelling the free and then we have the socialist engineering dictators, ruthless totalitarian control dragons and menacing old bears, big pharma agendas and topping it all off we have the rumours of wars.

What can we do then?

Yield, take His yoke upon us and learn His ways to be strengthened by the higher laws, fight the good fight and enter into His rest from the burdens.

I see the Light, shining into the darkness, removing the darkness, revealing lies and showing what the truth is. The light also lights us up, causes our whole being to come alive, to be activated to be how it is meant to be.
Is the light within dim and faulty? Be transformed.

I see the Love of God igniting cities, nations, turning people away from conflict and creating people brand new, like waking up into a day that is full of bright sunshine, where you have the love life to the max.

I see the Peace of God that passes understanding taking away hopelessness, depression and despair, healing mental illnesses, setting the people alight, now life is good and they know God is good.

Psalm 27.
The Lord is my light and my salvation;
Whom shall I fear?
The Lord is the strength of my life;
Of whom shall I be afraid?
One thing I have desired of the Lord,
That will I seek:
That I may dwell in the house of the Lord,
All the days of my life,
To behold the beauty of the Lord,
And to inquire in His temple.
For in the time of trouble,
He shall hide me in His pavilion;
In the secret place of His tabernacle,
He shall hide me;
He shall set me high upon a rock.
And now my head shall be lifted up above my
enemies all around me;
Therefore I will offer sacrifices of joy in His
tabernacle;
I will sing, yes, I will sing praises to the Lord.

In this Psalm, King David is set alight and saved by the Lord from defeat, King David is elevated above in a position of authority given to kings by a relationship knowing His God is faithful to deliver. King David is in God's presence which has lifted him into the place of security, in the high places far above the troubles of this world. Yes troubles are still coming, in this world you have troubles, but God delivers us from the fiercest of storms.

King David lives in the light of God.
King David can see beyond 2020 Vision and you can too.
I am reminded of the vision that the Apostle John had when he encountered Jesus as written in the *Book of Revelation.*

Jesus appeared in His glory and Majesty with a two edged sword coming out of His mouth.
In *Hebrews 4* there is mention of the sword that divides spirit, soul, flesh and the motivations of the heart; this sword coming out of His mouth will penetrate our entire beings and lay us bare, revealing all that is hidden and does not measure up.

Jesus is the Chief surgeon and healer at work in us to cut away all that isn't of Him and is bad for our overall health, He will prune and cut away which can be painful, but He will also bring healing by removing toxic and infected parts of us that leads us in to unhealthy choices and lifestyles.

One of the biggest threats to our overall health is negative emotions which come from wrong beliefs embedded inside causing us to react badly to situations, like a triggered response sending us into a spiral.

Fear would be the biggest one on the list, as it is opposite to faith, sends us on many wrong choices limiting our true potential.
Fear is a killer and when combined with nasty viruses can be a lethal combination if not treated correctly.

Fits of rage and out of control anger is a destructive emotion, we see this happening on the news and people are driven, they are not led by peace, which means they are out of control and that opens the door for evil spirits to come in take control of their actions. Deep debilitating depression and mental health conditions that just bring us down where we just can't function properly, this doesn't mean if we suffer from these we are stigmatised, this is a part of living in an imperfect world.
Also, addictions that usually are a result of negative mind-sets and the need for an escape from the constant barrage of oppressive feelings.

Jesus has come to give us life and life in abundance and that includes being set free from all these inner troubles that plague us in our battle for survival. Jesus came so that we don't just survive, we actually live in love, joy and peace, and we live the life of promise being more than conquerors.

The sword comes to bring inner healing of wounds that are festering, this is the healing side of the sword and then there is the other side which is more surgical cutting out, removing things, the dealings, probably the things that make us kick and scream, but this is for our own good and must be dealt with.

In the *Book of Revelation* Jesus is knocking on our doors, He wants us to be overcomers and be effective witnesses of His truth, as well as drawing close to Him and being a true friend, not compromised and also not having idols, other gods and ways that are contrary to His ways.
He is Lord of our lives and when we don't yield to Him then our interests are divided, you can't serve two masters, at some point one will be the dominant one, the one we give the most attention to will rule us, God help us all and He does.

That is where our help comes from, when we go to the throne of Grace to get the help we need to become overcomers in this life.

The Throne of Grace is mentioned in *Hebrews 4,* God provides a place to come to Him with our weaknesses exposed, when He highlights areas in our lives that don't measure up and we have wounds that need His healing touch, we find His mercy reaching out to us, He wants us to come into His loving arms of a Heavenly Father, this is where the exchange happens, our weaknesses for His strength.

Let the weak say they are strong, we find grace to help us in our needs to grow up into His image, to be more like Him and His ways.

Notice that there are two sides to the sword, which is the Word of God, Jesus is the expression of the Word, the Word of God is powerful, life changing, when it hits the mark we have one side bringing correction and the dealings, which is more about attitudes and wrong thinking and then we have the healing side by the removal of blockages and things that weigh us down and damage us emotionally and physically.

Kind of like two parts to the process, first the spotlight of the Word of God revealing our issues in the heart, if someone doesn't point it out we just carry on in the same mind-set driving over the cliff, God is kind and merciful He doesn't want anyone to suffer and then we have the mercy side where we acknowledge our imperfections, get help receive His help which is Grace to be living right, to become mature and better individuals, better futures.

The seven churches weren't perfect in the *Book of Revelation*, some however were doing pretty well but still needed to endure to the end, while others had issues that needed attention.
There was the False Prophet Jezebel controlling some believers, the Balaam influence of immorality and idols, the Nicolatians Doctrine of a mixture of Christian beliefs with worldly philosophies.

Then we have the loss of our first love; the church looking alive but is really dead, the Church of Satan in our midst, then finally the lukewarm church, all of these issues contain dire warnings to repent, sounds a lot like today doesn't it.

What does repent mean? Changing your mind, turning away from things that are no good.

I need to discuss further about what goes on with the sword dividing things, what is happening with this cutting, Jesus just isn't swinging wildly slashing everything like a samurai ninja. Jesus is about precision, His judgement is true hitting the mark with controlled strokes.

When Jesus is dividing, He is about separating targeted things from the whole, getting below the surface, getting to the bottom of things, seeing what is really going on inside, dissecting an argument, a mind-set, separating the lie from the truth or uncovering things exposing what is really there.

Jesus sees with pure fire and this is penetrating to the core, a refinement occurs, everything is laid bare nothing is hidden.

Our motivations need to align with the Kingdom of God, not some other agenda or selfish ambition.

Wrong mind-sets also include fear, fear that debilitates our faith, enslaving us to something or someone that is not from God, the fear of man, bowing down to the doctrines and the corrupt rule of man.

The enemy of our souls will use money, comforts of life and provision for our basic needs to enslave us into compromise or giving up our rights and principles.
Judgement begins with the house of God, but then it continues to the kingdoms of this world. Ideologies, wrong beliefs, philosophical arguments sound convincing and these like agendas are sold with marketing techniques to convince people to buy into it.

Deception only works if it is convincing, you need a good salesperson to deliver, great PR techniques, a charismatic politician to sell the plan if it is going to work.

A smooth operator will use propaganda, media editing and filtered content to give a particular point of view, statistics that agree with the argument or the narrative, get qualified experts that are on board or who have been bought, coerced into agreement with the plan, the usual party tricks.

Hello, we have been lied to! It's happened before in history and it will happen again, nothing new under the sun.
Buyer be aware, use discernment, do your due diligence, settle things in your own mind before you are sucked into the plan.
If the plan is idealistic, utopian better check it out, equality for all yes but at what cost and who will own you.

At the base of all alternative beliefs and philosophies is an attempt to replace the One True God and His values with other gods.

Just to be sure, God the Father, Jesus the Lord of all and the Holy Spirit who is revealing the truth.

You can't replace God, He is I AM, every other entity and person are creations trying to usurp and take illegal authority over others, so if someone is larger than life, where they are worshipped, idolised something is cock eyed, crooked, it's a scam, better run.

Check out the eyes, there is something lurking in there, spinning around, mesmerising like a snake, no good.

The aim is godly values upheld, the making of a good society, then fair systems in place like democracy, freedom for all as long as the rule of law is applied properly, freedom of speech, civil rights of the individual. Government is there to administrate these laws and principles for the people and not for the enslavement of people. We need to pray for all in authority that they rule correctly, like no killing of the innocent unborn.

Let's allow the Sword of the Lord to work in our lives, go to the throne of Grace when things get rough, get help, where the Holy Spirit is our helper, He is our counsellor to guide us through into being mature Sons and Daughters of God.

Finally after a process of refinement and trimming, the cutting away of the dead and the rotten, we will overcome and be established in strength and righteousness, we will become like the city on the hill, the light to the nations, arise shine, there is a lot of darkness covering the earth and you can see it on the news, His Glory comes, His Light shines, Christ in us is the Hope of Glory.

There is Good News and an answer for the world today.

The early and the latter rain, we get to see the miracles and the glory come, do the greater works as Jesus promised and commanded us to do, like casting out demons, healing the sick and uncommon miracles like multiplication of loaves and fishes, supernatural provisions, manna from above, endurance during impossible odds, what about deal with nasty viruses, you name it, He can do more than we can imagine or ask.

The master programmer is God the Father, Jesus is the Master Physician and the Holy Spirit executes the commands. The sword will divide down to our very DNA, this is where we will be reprogrammed and restored to the original design, and we will take on the image of Christ.

An image replicated creates a clean version, if the image created is then corrupted, then we need to go back to the master version, who is Jesus and rewrite the DNA code.

Corruption comes from wrong programs like viruses, pieces of rogue RNA interfering with the true expression and character, when this occurs we need a clean-up and restoration and this is what the sword of the Lord does, cuts out and removes corruption of the pure code. We are a New Creation in Him, purified from the invasion of corrupted malicious codes.

Be encouraged this is not a strange thing that is happening to us, we are all going through the stuff, weeping does endure for the night, the dark night of the soul, feels oppressive like we are so far away and lost touch with Him, the light at the end of the tunnel is there though it seems like a distant spot out of reach, we need faith and hope to drive us on, Holy Spirit fire takes us beyond the physical barriers, the vision will come, we must tarry for it, keep on believing, hanging on, yielding our lives and growing up in Him can be a challenging process, but in the end it yields a harvest of righteousness.

Now we can see that there is a coming great end time harvest and we are invited to be part of it, but also remember to be at work where we are at, one soul a time, line upon line, development of our character, like no one notices anything about us, but it all leads somewhere, upward to the break of day, the morning star arises in our hearts.

Joy comes in the morning.

God is interested in all souls being saved and the straying ones who have wandered off due to the challenges and temptations of life.

Matthew 18:12-13
New King James Version
12 "What do you think? If a man has a hundred sheep, and one of them goes astray, does he not leave the ninety-nine and go to the mountains to seek the one that is straying?
13 And if he should find it, assuredly, I say to you, he rejoices more over that sheep than over the ninety-nine that did not go astray.

This is how God feels about the lost, we can be part of His heart and feel with Him. When we see a straying one, we can have His heart towards them, pray for them, comfort them, encourage them, you haven't been in their shoes, show compassion and do whatever it is in your influence towards them to reach out and lend a hand.
If you are the lost sheep, know that He hasn't forgotten you, you are utmost on His mind and He is pursuing you to bring you back into the fold.

Look into the vision. Three WW2 ace airplanes, Spitfires flew overhead and passed triumphantly three times in Auckland July 2020.
What a vision to behold.
Sense of youth and exuberance and something from an older generation coming back to life.

We are resurrection life into victory no matter how young or old we are, we can soar, fly like eagles with precision and skill, we are overcomers in this life.

To be or not to be that was the question!
To be is the call.
To be is our response to the call.
To not to be is being robbed of the call.

To see is our response to the call and no longer be blind, to not to be is remaining blind.

Beyond 2020, we will respond to the call.

Seeing beyond 2020 Vision.

Things are looking very bright.

Amen.

Chapter 9

The State of a Nation

Victoria.
Victoria is no longer a state it is in a state of disrepair.

Setting a pattern.
Preconditioning.
Takeover.
Loss of Civil Rights.
Agenda 2020 - 2030 - whatever 1984!
This so called democracy is more like a totalitarian state of disaster!

Biggest loss is AFL Aussie Rules no longer played in the foundation state, gone!
Been shifted to the mates in QLD and all due to the bungled management of the manufactured bat bug, is this the convenient tool to carry out the agenda by chief comrade who is obeying orders from commander comrade?
AFL gone that should wake you up!
Seriously loss of business and huge debt to exist by the handouts, citizens becoming dependant no longer financial viable an easy takeover.
You always need thugs to enforce illegal takeovers.
Militarised Police Force.
What is Melbourne a Strong New World City Utopia?
Some Think Tank Revolution, a Revolution with hidden New World Order Strategic Agenda.

The song *"I put a spell on you"* at work here. People sheeple are spell bound, it sounds so good!
Just turn up the heat slowly on the frog in the boiling pot, gradually change from healthy environment to fatal environment, the frog hasn't got a clue, the frog isn't dumb he just looks dumb, just gets used to these subtle changes, shifts from Mr Shifty, all is well keep on swimming in the murky waters, the good master # I support Big Daddy Dan he is looking after me.

In a democracy where we have decent values, the Police are to be respected and obeyed, they do a great job when they are governed properly without corruption.
You can't blame the police for corrupt leadership, they are just following orders!!!

Power corrupts corrupt rulers!
Not saying the answer is breaking the rules, disobeying the law, use wisdom, however man's laws can be challenged is it really legal?
Vote for justice, vote for values, pray and speak Gods will be done!

You need justice with values, you need law enforcement based on values, and you need capitalism and business with values. We are blessed to be a blessing to others, yes capitalism based on greed and control is corrupt, but that doesn't mean the solution is totalitarian socialist control of the masses.

Find wisdom, take action whatever God reveals
for you to do.
Deficit! Deficit! Deficit!
My question is to any Government which has the
expertise to forecast the future state of the
economy, why would a Government allow such
an economic catastrophe and devastate the
future of their citizens?
Deficit - the excessively continued wage
subsidies long after we know the true effect of
the virus.
Deficit - businesses going bust and not able to
operate anymore.
Deficit - when wage subsidy runs out employees
no longer can work due to their employers
businesses gone.
A bankrupt state.
Who would bail it out?
A big bad superpower Boss Hog, but with strings
attached they now own you.
Welcome to the real world, enslavement.
What reason would there be for this plan?
Do the math.
Takeover.

You say because of COVID.
What that virus created in the lab and
deliberately released to cause economic ruin on
the west, upset the election outcome, any other
reason?
Oh yeh you have an arrangement with them.
Read the scientific report released by Chinese
virologist Li-Meng Yan.
Oh yeh don't forget you have an arrangement
with them.

CDC report that states this virus seriously effects less than 1% of population.

Oh yeh but the arrangement with them.

Sweden in herd immunity without closing down the economy and making its citizens suffer and this is from a Socialist Government.

Oh but they don't have an arrangement with them!!!

Even George Orwell supported Socialism, but maybe he had second thoughts about it when he listened in on the plans of the Elitist Fabian Society - 1984 Big Brother totalitarian control of the masses, de-population of the masses, with the added Gates Jab New World Order tracking tatoo.

In the UK 16,000 deaths were caused by the lockdown due to depression, lack of usual health testing for serious conditions like cancer, oh but you say you are caring for people and then the other stressful financial pressures, so if anyone got this virus add stress and you got a cocktail.

You get self-righteously indignant when someone breaks the rules and supposedly puts lives at risk like walking on the beach, yet you don't seem to care about the effects of these rules on peoples wellbeing's and the deaths that did occur due to mismanagement on the vulnerable in rest homes, particularly bad when there is a proven cure HCQ and various other accessible and affordable cures unless you ban them.

How can we continue to justify these lockdowns
if it is causing so much harm to overall health,
economy and piling on the future generations
debt and adversities?
We go on about the saving of the environment
for our future generations, but now we are
running up a huge debt for the future
generations, but this is OK!!!
The only way we can justify these draconian
lockdowns and all of the ridiculous rules is if
you are a deranged madman or the only other
possibility is you have an agenda, you are taking
orders from higher powers to fulfil an agenda,
Brave New World 1984.

Dan's Super Computer has all of the answers to
life's problems.
The AI Quantum cooked up calculations must
be hooked up to the algorithm of the Agenda of
how to effectively shut down citizens from
functioning to the point that they become pliable
for a takeover, use models already utilised by
Big Bro monitoring, surveillance, drones,
suppression of freedoms and rights to conform
to the ideal citizen points system, all thinking in
a uniform way like test tube genetic clones in
drab uniforms, eventually they all will be
plugged into the internet of everything where the
hive mind will control the speech and acceptable
behaviour.

Hey I was born in Geelong.
C'mon the Cats! Sam Newman, aint he the
popular one, Gary Ablett, Patrick Dangerfield.
Lived a big chunk of my life in Victoria.

Grew up there went to school there, this affects me even though I am now overseas.

Perhaps I can see things and react, because most of the citizens have been slowly cooked by clever spells and propaganda.
Don't like to see the state become a penal colony, prison camp, but this time no longer Mother England running the ship a global monster on the horizon.

The polls say all is OK, maybe all of the hash tag tweets are from paid operatives influencing the minds let alone the media barbarian bombardments, but what if you are a struggling business owner and the pub has got no beer, what if you are in a rest home in your last days and the family cant visit, what if you are someone who doesn't accept the status quo, does research, asks questions, use critical thinking not told what to think?
People aren't dropping in the streets, dead bodies aren't piling up everywhere, bombs aren't falling from the sky, and we don't need to hide in the shelter.

Do your own homework, research or just look out the window, its everywhere, shape the minds of the masses, control the airwaves, take over from within.

Victoria used to be home. Something has now moved into home is now taking over home and is wrecking the home.

Disaster State of a Nation. Borders don't mean that you will keep it out. Just a test case for western countries for the big plan.

Red alert!!! Triggered keywords the drones are coming, thought and speech police 1984 Fabian Philosophies, Mr Orwell listened in took notes it was planned long ago playing out got technology now blockchain AI, DNA genome fixing are we cooked?

Not unless there is a greater power employed to displace the lesser power. Higher Power is God. Time to employ the angels, issue His Words release it see things shift change.

Don't be a sitting duck!
I saw a dead duck on the side of the road.
Made me think about fatality.
Not to take things for granted next time you are sitting carelessly on the fence.
Maybe the duck was taken for a ride you say, yes that is possible, but heading the wrong direction into a trap, equally bad as sitting transfixed with the sights lining you up for the shot.

What can we do?

Discernment, wisdom hearing a voice behind you saying this way walk in it.
There is a highway of holiness prepared and when the glory comes it will be the secure slipstream to get into.

Don't be a sitting duck!
As in the days of Noah.
The serpent lizard tried to corrupt the DNA of man to stop the Saviour entering the world as an uncorrupted man and now what about His return?

And now for an allegory, a play on words and a kind of a satire, just a made up scenario to make a point, read the following - news flash!

This is a Covid Alert about the spread of a fatal pandemic by a deadly infected golf ball.
Did you know that if you play golf there is a high risk that you could kill someone with the virus?
That's right, we are basing this on strong scientific evidence using golf ball projection models from super computers, as well as advice from experts in disease transmission by projectiles, our findings clearly show that the virus can become air borne forming a viral cloud when blasted into the air by a whopping slog by these irresponsible golfers.

This is a serious threat that we are facing right now to our state and well-being, which is the possibility of being struck by a stray or targeted infected golf ball.
This is due to some irresponsible and sometimes enraged golf players engaging in this illegal activity.

This is particularly disturbing at this time during a pandemic as the golf balls have been shown to increase the spread of the virus.

The following is information and the background into what led up to this growing threat to society and the effects of the golf ball infection, infection numbers, including a scientific detailed explanation of how this phenomenon occurs linked to the spike protrusion of the golf ball.

This is going on right now, the state that we are in is terrible and we need to take action immediately before things get way out of control. It has been revealed through intensive analysis that the spike protrusion of the golf ball has been enhanced in golf balls manufactured and enhanced in a specialised lab with a gain of function ability.

The virus will also gather on the spike protrusion and when struck with particular aggression by the perpetrators will create airborne virus clouds that are increasing the spread over large regions where the golf balls have been struck by the unlawful activities of these alleged offenders.

Read on you just won't believe it, it could not be true surely but yes things are that bad.

Therefore if you live within 5 km from a golf course you may be at risk of catching the covid from enraged crazed rogue golfers protesting the enforced rules and out to prove a point.

These crazed individuals without a care for anyone else other than their own handicap, will stop at nothing to drive their point home.

The good news is that they only can play the game in daylight and we know for a scientific fact that the virus is only active after 8pm or in the case of daylight savings it will make the calendar adjustment to 9pm, so this means unless they play under powerful night lights and risk a huge fine and being spotted and chased down tackled to the ground by some law enforcement militia in combat uniform. Therefore you will have minimal chance of catching the virus from a loose golf ball smacked into your vicinity, breathe a sigh of relief and say a hoorah for our chief and commander comrade Dan for all of his careful attention to the critical details to combat this virus.

These inquiries looking into our handling of this deadly pandemic and criticisms from the odd alternative media are just a lot of fuss most likely driven by these fringe conspiracy closet golfers that have no real appreciation of elimination strategies, don't they know that sensible managed minimising and prevention is not enough, we need to get tough and blow the stupid economy to kingdom come if need be and forget about peoples mental health, we can keep throwing federal money at the economy anyway and besides we are all crazy here so what difference will it make if we are driven more crazy.

I am so glad that there are places in this world where we crack down on irresponsible people. Thankyou Dan and from the hash tag support Dan Brigade, we all just need to say you are my hero, you have saved us from well who knows what something bigger that what I can think about and you put Victoria on the road map, ride the North East link into the red sunset, forget the trams take the Chinese train, Victoria is world famous and Melbourne is such a strong city unless you are a business owner, well you can all buzz off, complainers, what is this being financially secure, we got handouts to Africa just line up.

Take control Dan, take control of the silly masses, just subjects what do they know they need your leadership, do the thinking for them take away resistance it is futile, the borg hive mind got the right idea.

Just get the jab, stop whining won't hurt puts a tracker in you better surveillance, we will know when you cross the red line over 5km, you crooked criminals.

Dan's leadership style reminds me of a movie called cable guy.
Where the deranged cable guy jokes about fining his new found friend $5000 and sending him off to the state penitentiary, like in the proposed police and prison state. Just as we find out later in the movie with the cable guy hooking us all into the super highway internet of things, this is no joke, Dan is either your best friend or your worst nightmare.
Dan will know if you are his friend by the secret handshake test.

By complying with the rules we have just made one more sensible step towards elimination. Elimination of what???

It will be all worth it, no stray golf ball will come anywhere near your household and infect you, danger danger Dan Da Man warning warning.

News Flash!!! Virus mutated from night time infection to 24 hours infection, the virus has had an update and a patch to operate easily 24 hours and therefore, the curfews are no longer of any use to management.

If these criminal golfers want to inflict injury on the innocent public, who are basically sitting ducks and will be picked off one by one by some infected golf balls projected in their general direction, remember the air borne molecular particles of this virus has a long range and can be like a cluster bomb effect on its victims covering a broad metropolitan area, so don't try running although you should be wearing a mask which offers massive protection over the whole of your mouth area, possibly an umbrella will also offer some protection as well, this has not been fully tested as we do not have many willing volunteers, but we may be able to trial this on the general public for the common good of all since the virus itself is mainly a social experiment so why not!!!

The other fortunate thing is that we have kept the 5km rule in place and this should restrict the golfers from accessing golf courses, but of cause *we are very generous with the public as they can now go on nature walks in the national parks and get much needed fresh air and exercise if they have a national park within 5kms of their residence, you know if you stray from this there will be a $5000 fine completely justified, I don't care if you are in the Simpson desert we will get you and you may infect the explorers in the desert like burke and wills you selfish thing you!*

Even if the golfers use their own mini golf course and send projectiles of which some are believed to be directed at parliament house they have no appreciation of all our hard work, we have devised new legislation for some of our trained public servant thugs militia brigade, maybe a few spare underground Boss Hog Comrades army officers could be handy to arrest these golfers and if they suspect that you are even thinking of doing these crimes they also have the power to detain you indefinitely, a menace to society must be removed, we need conforming programmed indoctrinated happy people to be part of our overall program and all will run smooth and be happy, no golfers permitted in the new normal, we will send you to special retraining camps to be model citizens of our brave new ordered strong city world.

We also have an idea who the possible ring leader of these resistance group of golfers is, none other than the former AFL Star, angry at us for no apparent reason, we just can't recall any reason, yes he is none other than Sammie Snapper.

Dan says we are on to him we got the surveillance, drones are on to him, he thinks he got away with it but we know what he is up to, we know that he purchased large quantities of golf balls on eBay, ha ha we are too good, no one escapes our ever watching eye, that is you know that eye in the pyramid thing, I think Dan can go all the way to the top of this pyramid thingy the way he is going.

Whoops there is another tin foil hat wearing former AFL player whistle blowing conspiracy person warning about corruption and all sorts of hidden things, how did Gary Ace know? Did he get inside our think-tank, he doesn't know the handshake does he?
This golfing activity is now getting out of hand and then there is also the people going to a beach on a beautiful hot spring day, what do I say, "oh golly gosh gee wizz, just stay home and follow the rules why don't you and I don't recall any reason why you must do that except that those are the rules".

Dan Da Man he got a handicap 666.
If you are thinking of leaving our state, great all part of the plan, our strong city will be populated by model citizens from the globalist population. This is the super city, super strong city utopia we have rules in place like no other except maybe our sister cities with our mates Kim and Xi.
Remember I can be your best friend or your worst enemy. Elimination of the nasty virus called "Victoria in the lucky country of the free", is the plan.

Hope you get the picture from this crazy golf ball or goof ball allegory.

Victoria don't be a victim, be victorious. Don't be a sitting duck!
The State of a Nation Victoria.
Be a free individual not a mind controlled slave to the system.
Freedom doesn't mean lawlessness as we are meant to have boundaries.

There is ONE that we should conform to, His name is King Jesus and we need to conform to His image.

What happens if there is a void?
Something will fill the void. Something foreign and dark is filling the void, unauthorised entry.
If you replace God with something else then this is dangerous and an opportunity for takeover.
Who has bewitched you?
Dan Marx.

Void of God, replaced by a philosophy becoming another god, it is the doctrines of men, but behind the mask it is the doctrine of demons.
You think a dynamic man is in charge, reality check it is a nasty commo gremlin talking through the dummy.

Don't be fooled there is a better way and it is up to you to choose wisely.
Repent turn from your wicked ways, return to the Lord and He will heal your land.

The State of a Nation, Victoria don't be a victim,
be victorious, you are not destined to be a sitting
duck.
When the Glory comes and the Good News is
declared with signs and wonders choose life.

If you want to live the rest of your life in a
lockdown until the planned whatever happens,
then this is the place to be, imprisonment,
slavery to a system comes to mind.

However, Australia has a destiny, it has been called the Great Southern Land of the Holy Spirit and that is how it is going to be.

I, Captain Pedro Fernandez de Quiros, hoist this emblem of the Holy Cross on which His Jesus Christ's Person was crucified and whereon He gave His life for the ransom and remedy of the human race. On this Day of Pentecost, 14 May 1606, I take possession of all this part of the South as far as the pole in the name of Jesus. From now on, these islands and lands shall be called the **Southern Land of the Holy Ghost** *to the end that to all the natives, in all the said lands, the holy and sacred evangel (the Christian Gospel) may be preached zealously and openly.*

Taken from published Historic Information.

The concluding chapters are about the clash of opposing kingdoms currently at war on planet earth and how the wealth of the world can be used for good intentions or bad. Really it is all about the souls of men and whether their gifts will be enslaved by darkness and be instruments for destruction, or if they choose the light they will be contributors for society and not against society.

Remember, this is primarily a judgement against the entities and the voice given to the persons, these hidden spirits operate through Government leaders and representatives enslaving them for wicked purposes, they are the controlling forces that oppose the welfare and future of all on planet earth.

It is Gods will that all should be saved, He wants all to repent and stop their wicked ways living a new life.

All of the devils toys can be free of the enslavement to wicked works and repent and be saved.

We were all like that in one way or another until we come to our senses and are saved.

God wants all Nations on earth to to be delivered from the darkness and be saved from destruction.

The Great Southern Land of the Holy Spirit will be saved.

The Great Southern Land incorporates the southern region in the pacific, Australia and New Zealand and the Pacific Islands Region.

You know vegemite sandwich country. (Let the reader research)

The author is passionate about these, place of birth in Victoria, Australia and now a resident of New Zealand (the land of the long white cloud).

Chapter 10

The Tale of Two Kingdoms

Prelude and some explanations of my writing style and methods used, a COVID 19 implementation plan.

These are the posts recently submitted on the Social Media Platform Facebook leading up to the post The Tale of Two Kingdoms, which is the main title of this article in the ongoing saga of 2020 as all of the events play out on the world stage.

Also note the style of writing is geared towards getting my posts past the Facebook censoring and filtering algorithms. This means you can't just come out and say what is happening in a straight talk fashion, even if you verify it or source it to reliable information. If it doesn't comply with the Facebook Narrative and filters of what they want you to believe is true then it will be dismissed, but also you need to go through some hoops to offer political opinions or controversial opinions that can be posted with a disclaimer.

Disclaimer: everything I have posted assumes you are an adult who can be grown up enough to do your own research, verify the claims or opinions, I am not assuming that my posts are to be blindly accepted, it is my opinion and my insight and what I believe should be written and broadcasted.

I believe we are still in a democracy and we can all form our own opinions after following a critical thinking diagnosis of the information received, not everything you read is true, duh so obvious no need to mention really, I assume you are not just being told what is and you can make up your own mind. And it is OK to have a differing opinion, this is not a dictatorship, where you have to accept what I say or be cancelled and bullied into submission, you are free to decide and accept or reject the views expressed here.
https://www.facebook.com/PeterKorenEBooks

I have attempted to go through the process on Facebook to add disclaimers with political and social views, but this has been in review since June 2020.

I just found out that there is an issue with my ID, although it passes the requirements, or perhaps it is the COVID 19 delays mentioned or something to do with November 4th ruling temporarily stopped running all ads about social issues, elections or politics in the United States.

Anyway it means some of the posts in this book were rejected by Facebook.
Now the rejected posts are only the ones that have been boosted to an audience in the AD Centre, so they were published but rejected by Facebook and will have a very limited audience.

The unboosted articles were not submitted for review and are usually the shorter posts for those who just happen to read everything on my Facebook page.

So from the beginning starting with *The Pyramid Scheme* I used a lot of like parabolic language, enigmas, symbols, alternative names, some fictitious riddles and satires with hints and clues to get the message out and hopefully pass the filtering and censorship rules of the Facebook Media Machine and mostly it worked, although *The Ruse* about the CCP Virus got rejected as well as *The Story of a very Selfish Dictator!!!* about our hero in Victoria, Dictator Dan.

This pattern continued like in *The State of a Nation* article and others following were also rejected for boosting. *The State of a Nation* is about what is occurring in the State of Victoria in Australia and what is behind this State having the harshest and longest lockdown in the world. Even though the death rate per million is about 35 at the time of writing and the case numbers which is more questionable data and what the media like to use in their scare campaign is comparatively very low, compared to the rest of the world hot spots.

They would argue that it is because of these harsh lockdowns that the numbers are down; but no that is not true, the State of NSW did not have harsh lockdowns and managed and traced their outbreaks efficiently and haven't got the issues like Victoria and did not ruin their economy and violate human rights and punish their citizens like Dictator Dan.

Also note the virus kind of has magically disappears when you want to go out and celebrate the election of the preferred candidate *(like where Dan's mate is in QLD)*, or protest climate change or the other socially correct protests.

Protest the lockdowns and the draconian rules and lookout the full force of the police state will come crashing on you and knocking on your door even after midnight.

Why has the Premier earned all of these names like Dictator Dan and Comrade Dan, because of his close association with the CCP of China with the Belt and Road Program and then following their practices of controlling, monitoring their citizens, using drones, surveillance, police state brutality and harsh fines with massive cover ups and corruption in their Government practices.

Why have I focused and picked on Victoria? Well for starters I was born there, I went to school there.

We are seeing the demise of democracy, personal liberties and freedoms challenged by a Global Big Brother Machine Agenda with Socialist Orwellian Surveillance and control over free speech as well as the shutdown of Western Economic Freedoms to be financially secure, with a push towards the state for financial supply and control.

The Governments are meant to be serving the people and for the people, elected by the people in a fair and democratic society and not adhering to Totalitarian Controlled Regimes practices that I believe are rolling out on the populations of the world. These agendas are Globalist New World Order nefarious plans to control everyone on the planet, run by technocrats and elitist billionaires empowered by dark occultic ancient societies that are governed by satanic forces to enslave all on the earth under their evil control.

The State of Victoria run by a control freak Premier Dan Andrews in Australia, is a glaring example of a supposed western democratic country that has embraced the CCP and its practices turning into a Big Brother, 1984 Orwellian, Totalitarian controlled Socialist Communist take over of the citizens, by this state controlling regime.

Then we famously now have the USA Elections playing out, I don't have to say much here. It is all happening in some kind of process to come to a true result. Do you want the democracy of the world going under the CCP Socialist New World UN Agenda 2030 Order, or do you want to hang onto your democratic freedoms and human rights?

If there is a problem, be the solution not an even greater problem to solve.

Do you think riots, destruction and anarchy by crazed ultra-mind controlled individuals corrupted and trained by warped ideologies is this the answer to how to fix the problems of this world?

If it wasn't for the suspect billionaires funding the chaos and the Marxist infiltration into the institutions that shape the minds of a generation, we wouldn't have the mad max army roaming the streets making a point by destroying the place, what happened to a healthy debate in a democracy and building towards a better future for all?

Be a contributor to society not a destroyer of society, where is the good in that?
It is the spirit behind these attacks and the driving force that motivates hate and destruction.

They want to dehumanise all to conform to thinking and acting the same way, this so called freedom which is really slavery and is the loss of individuality, true identity, loss of morals and a sense of what is right, creating love less machine digital like emotions, programmed clone like pawns on the chessboard of the cruel dark puppet masters.

Godless and lawlessness.

Calling evil good and good evil.

If it wasn't for our Heavenly Father and our God and people who are in the light who are praying effectively, we would all of being destroyed by now or turned into reprogrammed DNA altered part humans part zombies with dark souls existing on the planet, controlled by the few ultimate controllers and human handlers doing the work of their evil master.

There is Good News and I give thanks to an awesome mighty God who is love and justice and cares for everyone and doesn't want anyone to perish, we can all have a choice and choose life not death.

There is no judgement here, as all have a choice to turn and repent and be saved by a Good God who created us and sees our true potential and the better plan, who sent Jesus to be our sacrifice to save us, transform us into a new creation and set us free from our evil ways.

So the focus is on the players on the world stage in the big picture events with all of the related agendas including the Covid 19 virus unleashed as a bio weapon to bring down the democratic freedoms of the whole western world and eventually inject everyone with some RNA DNA altering, so called cure that will put a digital tracer on all like a mark, need I say more.

Is this the great tribulation talked about in the Book of Revelation?

It certainly has all of the markers and the ingredients to make up the potion of dehumanisation, loss of human rights and identity to the submission and worship of a supreme new world order system.

But there is the Trump Card being played right now and we will see where that goes all the way into the Supreme Court.

There is also a Supreme Court that is in Heaven and that is where judgments are decreed and Justice will be served and I really hope and believe that our time is not yet; we still have grace and mercy before those great and terrible times of the tribulation to reset and have a reformation to become the mature sons and daughters of God manifested on earth.

I believe the plan of God is to release these matured and empowered sons and daughters of God to be the harvesters of a Billion Souls plus on earth who will be delivered from the darkness in the great end time harvest when the Good News is preached to all with power and authority in the greater works that Jesus wants us to display in Love and Power in the Character of the New Nature that He purchased for His Special People who are Kings and Priests who rule and reign with Him; their lives inflamed with His purpose and authority to see His will being done on earth as it is in Heaven. This is an Elijah Generation and a spotless bride appearing in the preparation for His return to establish the Millennial Reign and Restoration of all things.

That is where we are, in the process of being aligned and refined to be who we are meant to be as He is so are we on the earth.
Jesus went about doing good and freeing all of those who were oppressed by the devil and He came to destroy the works of the enemy which includes devilish viruses.

He was anointed to set the captives free and we are being conformed into His image and represent Him within our sphere of grace gifts and authority that we are given to be His will on earth.

The following is a collection of posts prior to and leading up into November 2020, with the Election and all of the shenanigans under the sun.
Today is Nov 11th 2020 and we don't have the final outcome yet, but it is beginning to play out.

The Story of a very Selfish Dictator!!!
What is the definition of selfish?

A dictator that is all about their own agenda before the people he is meant to serve and protect.

A dictator that creates laws that harm the welfare of his citizens, remove the rights of the citizens, harm the economy of his citizens and then he fines and arrests his frustrated citizens that don't conform to his oppressive laws, while turning a blind eye to some that break the rules that he selfishly feels that suits his agenda.

A dictator that controls the airwaves of the media to program the minds of his citizens with biased propaganda that is his agenda while squashing and debunking all that oppose him and not allowing free speech that would be democratic and fair.

A dictator that outlaws the very cure to the crisis that was manufactured in a lab from the country that he is subject to, and allowing the crisis to spread into where the most vulnerable elderly and immune compromised are which will inflate the crisis, as well as selfishly not allowing proper support when offered, not submitting to better managed oversight, selfishly his inflated ego would not allow a cure to happen that would end the whole sick plan.

Dictator Dan thought he was the man, but all he could do is pull the wool over people's eyes and mismanage the garden state.
The weeds are getting in and taking over.

He is driving the state into the roadmap of ruin. But if you asked him about the inconsistencies, corruption, failures, incompetencies, he would reply, "I can't recall".

That is just what I see, but hey I am only reporting what I think is behind the curtain where you will find the Wizard of OZ, the little man with a loud megaphone broadcasting cunning delusions.

What's your views? That's fine we can differ, that's free speech in a democracy, I don't hate anyone because they see things differently, we can all live and learn from each other as long as we follow common sense rules that do no harm and inform in the right way whether someone likes it or not, it isn't about pleasing everyone.

Guess what we were all born convicts and we all can turn around, even Dan can and I pray that he will come to the realisation that he is not the one that is ultimately in charge, he is a slave, a pawn, a useful tool and behind the human mask is unseen evil entities and they are really in control of the dark agendas, but ultimately there is One that is Lord of all and Dan and everyone else and those hidden controlling dark beings must bow the knee to submit to the King of kings and the Lord of lords. We all must repent of allowing our lives to be directed by evil and even Dan can turnaround, his choice can be Dan the new man.

Choose Life!

Repent, enter into the way the truth and the life, when the Glory comes choose Jesus the King of kings and Lord of lords, there is no other way, no hero worship, no demi god man that can fix us, choose what is right and it will be a brand new bright day for Victoria.

Super Spreader Shepparton.

*A City in Victoria where an escaping Covid 19
infected truckie from the wall of steel surrounding
Melbourne the capital of Victoria in severest
lockdown, you know the story in country Victoria
where there has been minimal cases very few
deaths but still subject to harsh lockdowns.*

*This truckie allegedly causing the super spread
due to his travels, which if proper tracing was
used like NSW and just about anywhere in a
western country could have been minimised. Just
about all of Shepparton panicked when he visited
McDonalds and other spots on his rampage, fear
kicked in fuelled by the media, Lets all freak out
the virus has hit the town, lets all rush in and be
tested by improper unreliable tests, Dan how
could this happen you had the virus all locked
up? What a farce and big hoax we live in,
repeated advice, yes the virus exists take
precautions, HCQ oh yeh that is a cure that is
banned, OK other helpful immune boosters like a
lemon, then protect the vulnerable and we will
survive this pandemic flu without killing our
economies. Suckers. Well I am actually livid about
all this destruction, I went to school in Shepparton
grew up there, know the place well.*

So the Super Spreader in Shepparton did what?
Really!!!
This is more like a super stuff up.
Put into practice proper tracing of the infected
like NSW or just about anywhere in the world
that believe in prevention without ruining
society and this supposed spreader would not
have been allowed to roam Victoria willy nilly.

Super Spreader is the typical language used by the media to promote fear and panic.

That is how the people of Victoria are educated and taught what to think.

Which has resulted in the panic in Shepparton, that great city of my education at the infamous Shepparton South Tech School.

Great Mr Andrews you just delayed the inevitable, a super spreader virus created in the lab will hit your town sooner or later.

But now we know the death rate is less than 1% of the population, we have a year in 2020 where there is rarely any flu wonder why?

The tests for starters are grossly inaccurate, if you have had the flu shot it will most likely come back positive the test is only showing some RNA corona which has been around for donkeys years.

Has the Corona Covid 2 been isolated? This virus is highly contagious and spreads easily, that is how it was designed in the lab with gain of function, spikey.

So what should you do?

Really obvious unless you are a Government with a Global Agenda to control the population with lockdowns, ruin the economy make people fearful and dependent on the Nanny State which is really Big Bro State.

Protect the vulnerable, take precautions, take HCQ and Ivermectin and Zinc, get plenty of sunshine and exercise without a mask unless you in crowded places where it may help.

Don't rely on a vaccine coming, especially if it is a Gates special with DNA altering RNA including a micro tracing patch tattoo.
Don't rely on Suttons advice as he is a trained bureaucrat and trained professor of spin doctor. Rely on actually trained and specialised virologists, epidemiologists, independent ones not the ones paid by Andrews to say what he wants, have a listen to 500 doctors in Victoria that are actually treating this virus and getting results.

Also don't panic, this virus is a spreader yes, notice the case numbers spike, but the deaths are still about 1% and these are over 80s age group mostly in rest homes with other conditions who are supposed to be protected.

Don't rely on Andrews he gets his orders from the big boss hog with an agenda for the gateway into Australia through Victoria.

Dan da Man you are screwing it, but you are getting away with it for now, you got layers of protection sack everyone around you, don't recall anything, but as with all things it comes around, the truth will come out on the day of reckoning.

TRUMP.
Why Trump?

Because he is Gods choice.

Pro Life, Pro Family, Pro Values, Pro Justice, Pro rule of law, Pro free enterprise not shutting it all down, Pro healthy economy and business for the good of all and healthy neighbourhoods. Trump is the right choice. Pro Democracy.

It was reported that even after the lockdowns and the attack on the US economy by the virus the US economy rises in 'single biggest surge in American economic history'.
We need a problem solver not a problem maker.

This is the reality of the current Victorian CCP Centralised Control Party. How is that currently a viable management and where is the collaboration and consultation, I thought we progressed beyond out dated systems of management for Government in Democratic Countries?

What is the assumption? That the leader is a god type figure that rules with absolute authority that can't be questioned! It assumes that the leader is the only one who is right and doesn't listen to sound advice from experts even if they are more qualified, more experienced and more in touch with reality of the running of say business or the future economic impacts of decisions made.

Experts who have expertise in peoples immune system health and mental health wellbeing are shut down in favour of one who thinks he knows better for whatever questionable reason.

Goodbye democracy and being free to being under a totalitarian control Police State who hands out extensive fines to finance their agendas. Soon AI algorithms will decide how you will behave, at the moment it seems that the people's opinions are just being monitored and manipulated.

See Beyond 2020 Vision. You will see what's going on behind the mask.
It is about the values brothers and sisters. It is about the values. It is not about the personality, don't pay attention to that, vote for values, and your vote counts. Make a difference, vote correctly, righteousness and justice you will have the backing of Heaven otherwise you are choosing Hell on Earth. Choose life, Heaven on earth as it is in Heaven, Gods will be done, His Kingdom Come.
I have designed the superior performance verified alternative solution for face masks to combat the virus. You cut out a hole where your mouth is and start declaring and decreeing *Psalm 91* and other faith statements, we are not given a spirit of fear but of power and love and sound mind. Be bold and courageous like Joshua and speak out what God has promised and the walls will come down! We are not conformed to the pattern of this worlds thinking, our minds are renewed and we trust in the Lord and do not turn aside to the lies. Jesus went about doing good healing all those who were oppressed by the enemy. Jesus told us to do the greater works and not bow down to the system of this world!

In case you have to wear a mask where there are these rules from the big chief chairman, put in a Velcro stick on piece where the mouth is to keep big bro happy.

Lies Lies Lies and more lies.

Let's talk about why certain people are selected for positions of power with great influence over others.
You have the used car sales person just using this as an example, you know like an Arthur Daly from the TV show Minder type personality, although he was amusing and a bit of a character.
Then you have lawyers you know like liar liar the movie.
Then tragically now we have certain politicians. Especially if what is needed is someone who is able to bare face lie and just carry on regardless while spilling out lies without any sign of remorse.
Hey I am influencing the outcome of a nation's future and what the hell that's why I am here!

Professional spin doctors, masters of deception, an experienced and long term practiced liar fits the purpose.
What about the sold out media paid to be a mouthpiece for the illusion, should we add these to the list? yeh I think so.

Rigged Nation.

There you have it that's how the game is played as the machine carries out all of the shenanigans under the sun, completely duping the public, you have the front man who stands out there as the bare faced liar, and he or she is chosen by the ability they have to keep up the appearances, convince the public that all is above board, while lying through their teeth with the whole nine yards of forked tongue trickery, a politician star is born, there is a sucker born every minute.

That's how they are hoping it's going to be and how they hope they will get away with it, no questions asked, no legal action.

However, that's not what will happen this time, there is legal action and the injustices to the outcomes will be exposed, lies will not prevail and there will be consequences and justice will prevail.

The Trump Card always wins.

Its straight forward Justice Truth and Righteousness, include equity which means fairness. All else is corruption and that leads to slavery loss of freedom and human rights replaced by tyranny to an evil system and the end of democracy replaced by 1984.

Remember the Movie called *"The Sting"*.
The Sting operation is back with vengeance justice will be served.

Isaiah 55
6 Seek ye the Lord while he may be found, call ye upon him while he is near:

⁷ Let the wicked forsake his way, and the unrighteous man his thoughts: and let him return unto the Lord, and he will have mercy upon him; and to our God, for he will abundantly pardon.
⁸ For my thoughts are not your thoughts, neither are your ways my ways, saith the Lord.
⁹ For as the heavens are higher than the earth, so are my ways higher than your ways, and my thoughts than your thoughts.
¹⁰ For as the rain cometh down, and the snow from heaven, and returneth not thither, but watereth the earth, and maketh it bring forth and bud, that it may give seed to the sower, and bread to the eater:
¹¹ So shall my word be that goeth forth out of my mouth: it shall not return unto me void, but it shall accomplish that which I please, and it shall prosper in the thing whereto I sent it.
¹² For ye shall go out with joy, and be led forth with peace: the mountains and the hills shall break forth before you into singing, and all the trees of the field shall clap their hands.
¹³ Instead of the thorn shall come up the fir tree, and instead of the brier shall come up the myrtle tree: and it shall be to the Lord for a name, for an everlasting sign that shall not be cut off.

The Tale of Two Kingdoms.

That is what is going on right now, there is an almighty clash of two polar opposite Kingdoms and it is one massive fight to the finish.
Like two wrestlers grappling looking to overthrow the other one and subdue them into submission.

We have like a King David taking on one huge and ugly Giant Goliath System.
This isn't pretty at the moment and the heat will be turned up and come crashing down on the party.
Fire and lightning will be thrown on the camp and it will be in disarray after its complex and crafty techno devices are revealed and disarmed.

We are translated out of the Kingdom of darkness into the Glorious Kingdom of Light.
We are no longer of the world but we remain in it right in the thick of the ongoing battle.
There is a table set with blessing right in the midst of our enemies.
The Kingdom is advancing and the violent take it by force.

No time to be neutral and disarmed, keep the armour on in readiness with shields up and sword drawn, stand your ground, stand firm.
What are our weapons, mighty for taking down strongholds?

Joshua had the people marching around the walls of Jericho seven days and then they sounded the trumpet.
Intercessors, prayer warriors, saints of God proclaim the victory and keep on standing on the day of battle.

The battle belongs to the Lord, we are seated in the Heavenly Realms far above any other authority, that's where we rule from above.

Resting in His power and strength and at the same time picking up the stone and slingshot of accuracy firing with deadly precision at the head of the Giant.

The giant who was boasting and speaking threats of intimidation, inflicting fear into those who stand for Values, Righteousness, Justice and Gods will being done on earth.
The big horrendous Nephilim beast of a giant was slain with one stone from one lad full of faith who dared to stand up against him, against all the odds he took him out with one blow and then cut off his head, his evil sounds and projections were cut off and silenced for good and the armies chased off the enemies who were soundly defeated from the position of overwhelming loss, contrary to all the evil reports the giant went down hard.

They will be hammered and the scorecard will now go against them.
Justice is coming.
King David was anointed and he rose up and defeated the giant.
Easy no way, this will be huge.
This is the ongoing tale of two kingdoms.

This article was published on November 9th 2020, just to give you the timeframe.

Here is the continuation posts following The Tale of Two Kingdoms.

Imagine This!

Election Integrity and the South Dakota Fair and Just Voting System.

Imagine a fair and just voting election system that is implemented like what Kristi Noem the Governor of South Dakota has used in the 2020 election.

No one reasonable disputes the results there.

A fair process that is transparent to the voting public and is authorised, legitimised and checked for irregularities and outright theft and cheating.

Observers from both parties given full and transparent access to the process.

No dodgy Chinese infiltrated Dominion Software easily hacked by operatives with votes being switched from dark locations.

Irregularities and fraud will be checked like dead voters, out of state voters, unauthorised voters, and altered votes. Manipulated votes and many more tricks, you name it they do it.

No late ballots, any mail in votes verified by ID and Signature checks.

Valid votes counted up to and before Election Day deadline.

No trucks arriving with thousands of ballots in swing states at 4am and counted after all observers sent home.

South Dakota, Texas and Florida and some others seem to have this sorted in varying degrees why not the other States?

Bring in a proper system ASAP and eliminate corruption, cheats and frauds, interference from Big Tech manipulation, all of these illegal votes should be disqualified and do not count.

With a proper system in place with strong penalties for corruption, should dissuade the outrageous and blatant cheating going on. Better for Democracy, better for the voting people of USA who want a fair and just result!

What counts on the day of reckoning!

What God says about a false count or measure!
Proverbs 11
[11] *A false balance is abomination to the Lord: but a just weight is his delight.*
Proverbs 20
[10] *Diverse weights and diverse measures,*
They are both alike, an abomination to the Lord.
Proverbs 20
[10] *Two things the Lord hates are dishonest scales and dishonest measures. Contemporary English Version (CEV)*
Proverbs 20
[23] *Divers weights are an abomination unto the Lord; and a false balance is not good.*
Proverbs 20
[23] *The Lord hates dishonest scales and dishonest weights. So don't cheat!*
Contemporary English Version
Proverbs 20
[23] *Differing weights are an abomination to the LORD, And a false scale is not good.*
New American Standard Bible

Whichever way you look at it, it isn't good.

Micah 6
10 Are there yet the treasures of wickedness
In the house of the wicked,
And the short measure that is an abomination?
11 Shall I count pure those with the wicked scales,
And with the bag of deceitful weights?
12 For her rich men are full of violence,
Her inhabitants have spoken lies,
And their tongue is deceitful in their mouth.

Seems God doesn't miss a trick, you can't pull
the wool over His eyes and He aint looking at the
News Media Reports on TV to find out what's
happening.

God can count and knows what you are up to
and He knows if cheating is going on and is not
happy about it!
Abomination is a strong word, which means
justice will be a strong conclusion!
Which means dire consequences unless you
confess, repent and remedy the outcome, which
is better for you and those effected by the
damages.

One way or another it will all come out in the
final count.

Chapter 11

All of the other things being Equal

Billionaires, Oligarchs and World Totalitarian Leaders are saying *"you'll own nothing and be happy!!!"*

Do you see the blatant contradiction? Billionaires and world leaders don't own nothing, rulers of totalitarian states don't own nothing.

They live well off at the expense of others and they live celebrated pomped up lives of self importance, sometimes hidden away in castles which are fortresses with armed militia guarding all their property and wealth, not to mention their handy millions in Swiss bank accounts and maybe a heap of gold bars stashed somewhere.

They don't own nothing and this is the inflated out of kilter contradiction, they have amassed fortunes and are living in luxury while espousing to the peasants and the masses to learn to be all equal, more like learn to be robbed and cheated.

Oligarchs and their pet gargoyles operating behind the scenes.

Fair dinkum this is one massive con job and we are being sucker punched out of our property and hard earned life savings.

The state won't give you much, just a pittance token for survival and a bowl of rice on a good day.

This is the deal! We grab it all from you, take away your goods and now you have equality, we will do that after we take away the guns so you don't resist.
We the elite class will manage all of the resources and be handsomely insanely rewarded for doing so, someone has got to rule and we have decided it will be us.
Elitist totalitarian Orwellian control what a plan.

Meeting in Davos or is it Davros like the king of the daleks.
So we will have zero carbon by 2050 and by that time most of the population will be eliminated if they get their way.
What about practice what you preach isn't that what you accuse the religions of the world with?

Maybe there are some good examples of outstanding human beings who lived this life for others.
Mother Theresa and Gandhi, various monks and holy people over time.
But they still will never come anywhere near what the true Saviour of Mankind has done.

Jesus Christ who is Lord of all, He came forsaking His sovereign rule to become poor in order that we might become rich. *2 Corinthians 8:9*

That is grace and mercy and is what true leaders offer.
Do you get that? He came to give all of us life and life in abundance.

Sons and daughters of God get a gold coin from the fish's mouth.

What a contrast this is to the proposed agenda 2020 - 2030 of whatever, the brave new stupid world utopian dream more like a nightmare. Maybe the hired thugs that go about enforcing the rules will get a bit extra for their cruel oppressions.

So they say, lets reset the worlds fortunes into the hands of the filthy few who will live like wallowing hogs while the rest of the sheep people go to the pits.

King David says I saw none of the righteous children begging for bread. *Psalm 37:25*

A good leader empowers their people into living a better life, not taking away their abilities and wealth in order to be so called being equal. The right way up is we are blessed to live life to the full and to have the ability and means to be a blessing to others.

Wisdom says long life is in my right hand while riches and honour are in my left hand. *Prov 3:16* Wisdom from above is peace and purity. Wisdom from below is demonic and is full of confusion and selfish ambition. *James 3*

There is a better plan for you and a better plan for me.

There is a great overturning coming, this is not the planned great reset but an overturning of corrupt verdicts and practices.

No more unjust weights and measures will be tolerated and the lies will be exposed, justice and equity will have the final say on the outcomes.
I see dominoes falling and tumbling down.

Choose life.

Chapter 12

The Talents

Is God a capitalist?

Well He certainly is not a Socialist!

God doesn't go around calling everyone comrade, God doesn't create us all into a production line of robots, dressed up in the same drab uniforms and who look the same and act the same in robotic fashion. May look like you have a super soldier army, but the reality is it is dehumanising people, making them act like machines devoid of individuality.

We don't all have to think the same way and squash anyone who disagrees, why? Because life is about learning and no one has all of the goods, we are always learning something new every day and that is how it is meant to be even into eternity.

Free thinking and critical thinking is like wisdom and discernment, discovering what are the best paths and not being uniformly programmed by someone's so called superior system, which is totalitarian state control in cahoots with elitist techno billionaires who want to inject you, alter your DNA and implant a wireless traceable chip. That is a very dangerous controlling form of arrogance and pride and pride always comes before a fall.

God is love, He disciplines His sons and daughters as a perfect loving Father would.

God gives grace to the humble and resists the proud who think that they can command the world and make others subject to their programs.
Men and women don't need your programs, ideologies and philosophies that are the corruption of something uniquely made perfect at the beginning. What people need is to be empowered by proper mentors to be better contributing individuals made in the image of God.

God is all about encouraging and developing a person's potential for their benefit and satisfaction and for the benefit of others. All of us possess something worthwhile for others by our unique talents.

What is Gods idea? Multiplication, increase and an ability to create wealth.
God is not about negatives.

God's idea is to take away the negative and add in the positive and allow the transference to grow and multiply.
Take dominion and multiply on earth as it is in Heaven, God is into green OK! Green means go.

Sustainable yes, fit for purpose yes, but much more that, it is more than we can imagine and imagination ignited means power to get wealth.

Generation of wealth leads to stimulus of economies, which leads to more for everyone and abundance which goes around, like a stimulus package benefiting the community, the city, the nation, the world. That's how to get things going and flowing. I am in for that.

Socialism is so limited, unimaginative, lacks innovation and motivation, the only forward motion is from a dictator compelling people to do the agenda. Not much originality happens just a lot of intellectual theft from someone who has it. God is not limited and He doesn't want us to be limited either.

Plant the seed and cause it to grow, manage the increase and the left over to distribute and plant again, seed time and harvest time, this is all about the goodies for everyone according to how each one is gifted to be wilful distributors.

We are not cookie cut carbon copies, mass produced all the same which is the dumb and dumber solution that kills true potential and makes us all dull boys and girls, repetition is boring and we were not made to be like that.

Why is this dumb and dumber?

Because we didn't learn from history as it has already happened over and over before, there is nothing new under the sun.

Socialists, Marxist Communist takeovers leads to the destruction of society, employing armed militia thugs who are useful dispensable idiots who participate in the great loss of life, removal of enterprise and middle class prosperity, oppression of business owners, which results in extreme poverty to the inflicted nation and a lot of broken promises by the leaders.

When does socialism work? Never! The only way it simulates working is when it hooks into the capitalist free society and benefits from that society, in other words it makes a profit and competes in the free market which is a centre left mixture of socialism and capitalism, which of cause must remove the extreme totalitarian dictatorship rule. However, that is like having some benefits and then throwing in some obstruction, why would you do that?

Transition from one society to another, the gradual method to not disrupt the public too much causing a backlash and loss of power.

That is what we are experiencing in the democratic free world right now, some freedoms mixed in with some cunning transitional policies to take away our liberties and rights. A gradual decline into the abyss. However, notice some of these so called democratic leaders are displaying some dictator control tantrums, with ridiculous laws that squashes free enterprise and civil liberties.

Are we all headed into slave labour in sweatshop factories? That just isn't right either.
What good is it if it doesn't benefit all? Only the cream at the top get the privileges from the profits, the cream has gone off, the elite at the top of the pyramid get all of the privileges, while the common folk just survive or maybe move up a notch when things are running well.

Is the free world perfect? No it isn't, that's why this way of life gets challenged by ideologies, and they capitalise on the weaknesses of the capitalists and appeal to some disenfranchised groups to overthrow the whole lot. The baby and the bath water get thrown out and then they manufacture a carbon copy baby, a cheap copy fake version. One thing we will always have is boom and bust, the markets are not always kind, why?

The world is not perfect and there is corruption and an unjust distribution by the spirit who has mastery of the world that is Satan, he gives riches and rewards to all his puppets who do his dirty work.

Don't be a waste or be wasted.

The thief comes to kill steal and destroy, but Jesus came to give us life and life in abundance and that is the turnaround, the breakthrough, the revival of a proper dominion of this earth.

Yes it is Gods idea to have increase and He more than encourages making a profit on your investments, if you shrink back from what you have been given, God is not pleased and He will rebuke you.

You need to make use of the resources and abilities given.

We need His Kingdom to come and not the dark kingdom which leads to destruction with a lot of false promises and deceptive do good for all doctrines, which are cleverly marketed lies using a bombardment of propaganda through media and cancel cultures to anyone who opposes this onslaught.

The Parable of the Talents. *Matthew 25* Stewards of finances were entrusted with varying amounts and expected to bring back a return with increase. Notice that the stewards were given different amounts.

Does it sound fair when some are given more than others? Where is the equality in that?

However, he who is given much, is responsible over much. The steward given 5 talents made a 100% return and the steward who was given 2 talents made a 100% return.

They were celebrated as good and faithful stewards.

Whereas the steward given the least, he had the least to be responsible with and still he hid it away, he despised the gift and made nothing in return. He was rebuked as a wicked and lazy servant.

God is not into letting your talents be hid away to be unproductive.
Why?

The Kingdom needs working capital to proceed. God is into making more and being productive when it is used righteously, as this helps build a better society.

Here is a question about equality, if all were meant to be equal then there could not be a Chairman, as all would be the Chairman Premier god like figure that demands to be worshipped.

Think about your team of tradesman, not all are equal, you have a supervisor, some that specialise in one way or another. Some need to work harder to achieve the results, some are geared towards supporting the project.

However, all are a unique expression and no-one else can do things the way that each individual can. We are all called and gifted to make a difference. Some have more responsibility and therefore are more accountable, some are at different stages in life and haven't found their place for one reason or another.

Life is like that, don't try to change things to fit your agenda on how you think things should be, this world isn't perfect and the best we could do is find our unique place and contribute. Be the solution not the destruction of things, that's not how you deal with problems. Problem solvers improve the outcome, yes introduce change in a transition that doesn't harm society.

The Devil is a socialist as his ideology takes away any responsibility and any initiative to use your talent and increase it.

Notice we are not all on the same level, the gifts are distributed as God wills and He knows what is best for each individual and what they can handle.
Some are created to have more, but all are created to develop and improve what they do have and to be productive and be a contributor to society, with the priority to the Kingdom of God, His will to be done on earth.

Seek first the Kingdom of God and all of the other things will be added to your life. It is not about empire building, becoming a self-sufficient tycoon where you live a life for luxury and spend it all on your own pleasures.

It definitely is not about accumulating all of the riches and resources and controlling them with a monopoly in order to gain control over the populations. That is oppression.

We are blessed with the blessing of Abraham.
Jesus came to be the curse for us, because
Adam and Eve fell to Satan's devices in the
garden. We all went under the curse and became
a slave to Satan's rule on earth and he stole the
dominion of the kingdoms of the earth.

Man was entrusted to have dominion over the
earth from the beginning, but once we ate of the
tree of knowledge of good and evil, our eyes were
opened to the possibility of being our own god,
choosing whatever we feel is good or bad, we can
call evil good and good evil as we see fit, but
then we became a slave to Satan's rule.

Without God there is only one other rule and
that is Satan.

However when Jesus died in our place and took
the punishment due to us as sinners, we then
are all offered by an act of faith and our choice
to be translated out of the kingdom of darkness
into the Kingdom of Light where Jesus is Lord of
our lives.

We are blessed along with Abraham to be a
blessing to others on the earth.

The taxman. We do need to pay taxes, but they
are not meant to be a burden. *George Harrisons
Beatles Song, the Taxman* taxes just about
everything including the air, like carbon tax. Life
has twists and turns and snakes in the grass,
but Gods will is the crooked is made straight.

Don't think that if you have been given funds that you need to have a false humility about it, you are entrusted with riches, be wise with it. He gives us power to create wealth.

We are talking about surplus in this article, not your living expenses and providing for your family.

This is specifically about financial expert stewards, they are financial generators and managers who are given talents to invest and earn far above their living costs, they receive the wisdom like Solomon to be wealth creators on earth.

Abraham was our father of faith, Abraham had great wealth. That means it is OK to have the lifestyle that goes with wealth, you can enjoy the wealth, God is no meanie, He gives good gifts to His own, its Ok to own money and goods as long as they don't own you. There is the god of mammon to contend with.

God is not the big sugar daddy in the sky, with wealth comes responsibility, if you are given these talents He will also give you the ability to handle it.

In *Acts 2* they gave away their surplus as a free will offering for the purposes of God. That is how the money works.

You put it back into society, or you put it to work in investments and grow more, this causes circulation and a distribution flow to occur, like electrons moving through the wire. If you cut the circuit, you stop the flow and there is no power and the light bulb goes out, you then have no light and you end up in the dark.

Give it away, circulate it, what goes around comes around, you will see returns. Even like the widow with the two mites in *Luke 21*, these are like two pennies and it is all she had and she gave it away in faith believing God would look after her, not knowing how and not doing a formula, she was motivated by love and gave all she had, oh what a blessing awaits.

With a spring in her step she gave. Well that is using a bit of imagination license, but I am sure she felt the joy of the Lord when she gave.

Not a formula like I put in 1 and get 100 back every time guaranteed, you would go to a slot machine for that. God looks after you and He determines when, how and what comes back for your best and all things are working out for the good as you are called to His purpose and love God.

Witty inventions will increase. When people are blessed they have confidence to build more and distribute more, spending more as well as putting money into circulation.

There are better ways to spend money, it doesn't mean reckless spending, you need wisdom to manage wealth properly, with training and development comes maturity and you still need the seed to plant for more growth.
God provides seed for the sower.
What the world needs is wealth creation stewards, do you know any Government leaders who encourage that? They are the right one!!!

Socialists promote abortion, they kill babies, they abort what should be birthed. All wealth creation needs to be birthed and managed and brought to maturity. Socialist agendas steal and diminish potential, this limits healthy growth and growing a vibrant society.
When you grow produce, you don't want all of the fruit to be limited to a minimal size or less, that is a shrivelled up and miserable vision.

Choose life not death. Jesus came to give us life and life in abundance.
The Devil came to steal, kill and destroy, you can see which belief system is which. Unless you have been blinded to the truth and choose to exchange the truth for a lie to fit your own warped agenda, or you have been bought and paid for and serve your masters.

God's judgement is on those who have hoarded the talents. This means those that control the resources of the world and do not distribute for the common good of all, centralised control that takes away and impoverishes people is evil.

Yes that's right, the Kingdom of God has the final say on what is right and demands justice. God loves mercy over judgement, judgement is like a stop light saying don't go through onto the train tracks, the coming freight train will kill you.

He offers us a way out every time.
But for those who won't listen and refuse to do the right thing with the worlds resources there is the great transfer coming. No not the great reset to the money system no that is not the plan, the great transfer of wealth is.
There is the great transfer of the wealth of the wicked which will go to the righteous who will use it to help others and not harm others.

The meek will inherit the earth.
The silver and gold are Gods, that's how it is and will be, you can create a big load of paper contracts, derivatives, lease what's not even physically there, but in the end it will come back to bite you.
What comes around goes around, same with false ballots, it will come back to bite you one way or another, sooner or later.

This is not condemnation. This is not meant to say that you have missed it and now God will punish you.
It's not over.
The story is still being told.
It is how you finish that counts.

The stewards were at the end of their lives I believe and were in the day of judgement and had to give an account, as they now had to enter with whatever they finished up with into eternity.

You might have started on the wrong track, you may have chosen the easy road to destruction, but you can still choose the right path. You might have tried and got flattened by the waves of opposition, you might be discouraged with how the world operates robbed of your future and feeling ship wrecked unable to get back up again. Remember, it's not over.
His yoke is easy and His burden is light. Take His yoke upon you. He who began a good work in you will finish the course. We learn from life's mistakes, tragedies and opposition.

God is good, God gives grace to the humble, so that is those who are willing to acknowledge that they need God to live and do the right thing. Yes it is your decision, the choice is yours and then God's grace kicks in to bring you to completion of your story to be told.
The prodigals are coming home, the radicals are turning, the rebellious and the fools are getting hit by the light and they are changing their ways when they encounter the love, the light and the brightness of His coming, enter in with your dreams, enter in with your calls for help, enter in with your tragedy, enter in with your lost hope, enter into the new day and the new way and the new creation of His reality, which is your story to be told.

The gold and the silver are the Lords, perhaps some of those who hold the riches will acknowledge this and relinquish their control and be translated into the Kingdom of light from the kingdom of darkness.

God's mercies are new every morning and great is His faithfulness, when you become His sons and daughters and don't look back, you will move forward into where you will shine brighter like the new day sun.

Woe to those who refuse Gods will for their lives and only desire to control their wealth and control others by manipulation, control and deception.

Greater is He that is in us than he that is in the world, the promises belong to us and we will be wise and perform great exploits, shining like the stars of the universe we will be transforming communities, cities and nations with the Good News that Jesus came not to condemn anyone but to save them.

Distribution of wealth is coming as well as signs, wonders and miracles, with supernatural healings and creative miracles flowing to the needy.
Calling all of the intercessors and saints to keep praying, believing, declaring the promises of God, declare His will be done earth, justice is coming, reformation is coming for the great end time harvest of souls.

The thing is that we are all born like a fresh and clean slate and then what happens? Heredity and Environment.

We generational inherit those genes from the pool of what our ancestors got up to skeletons and all, DNA patterns weaved into our beings which gives us a bias like a leaning towards certain behaviours, we still have a choice and we don't have to give into it.

Then there is that pesky environment, all from this bad old world that happens to us, emotional, physical, psychological damage that is inflicted on our poor souls.

We still have a choice, do we react or do we respond to the negative dealings?

We are like that clean slate until like bad programs come along and infect our beings with a malicious code inserted into our DNA, which pulls us away from the original pure design. Now the slate is marred and scarred, marked and corrupted, who then can save us?

Thank God He always had a redemption plan for us, He knew we would all go astray one way or another, no one is perfected by the law, on the contrary we are all convicted and then remain condemned by the law.

All have fallen short, we all miss the mark, because we are marked and give in to the impulses and the reactions, we are drawn into to it, we are addicted to it, we lash out against it and cause harm.

Innocence lost we need to be rewritten.

The law of the Spirit of life sets us free from death.
The Book of Life contains all of the good things we are called to do.

We need the power of God, the light of the world and only He lights up all mankind with His life, He is the way the truth and the life. When we are led down into death, He is the life.
We don't have to continue to waste what we are given and use our God given talents for the wrong purposes. There is a good news ending to our story. Our story is not over, time to turn the page and start a whole new chapter, yesterday is gone, today can be the new day dawning.

The Dream.

I was in some sort of training special agent style, I was in a maze of buildings futuristic structures, a construct matrix. I needed to follow the right pathway to exit and reach the destination. I seemed to be headed the right way turning this way and that following my instincts. But I couldn't reach a conclusion and didn't see what the key to this highway was.

There was a lady also in training and she completed it and said to me, can't you see it? I was puzzled so I went back to the trainer supervising my mission. He said you are on the right track, now see the pattern you have followed from above.

What I discovered when I was given this insight from above was that I was following a shape through the matrix like a shape of a cross. Now I just needed to keep going with the wisdom from above which helps me understand what I am going through and complete the course to complete the mission.

Revelation is needed from above. Interpretation: the trainer is the Holy Spirit, the lady represents the spotless Bride of Christ. I am on a journey which is not completed yet. I need the right revelation to where I am going. We are on to it now. The Cross.

Have I arrived yet? No. Still a work in progress, being refined, got battles, some long term issues still dealing with. He began a good work and He will finish it.
Our real life is hidden from view looking with natural vision and how other people see us.
Colossians 3
Now we are actually declared dead by the great exchange, which means the old corrupted life is considered passed away and we get to trade in our old ways at the throne of grace and exchange our weaknesses for His strength in newness of life.

We just need to put on the new person who is the original design, like we fit those perfect clothes tailor made just right for us, looking good we are made in the image of God and not hacked into by a malicious attack, we are not cheap copies or junk.

We need to go through the cross, it is central to how we live and receive the resurrection life, which is the promise of the Spirit. Our spirit is alive, we have life and peace, Jesus just took that old life away and put it out in the trash, those dirty and smelly old clothes don't look so good.

How do we overcome the world and all of its trials? By our God given faith, if we are led by the spirit then we won't go down that dirty old track.

We are now on the road to somewhere.
Be blessed and be a blessing.

Choose Life.

Peace.

Chapter 13

The Valley of Berachah Experience

I want to talk about a valley experience and some battles won against all of the odds, especially when all appears to be lost. Have you been there does it sound familiar, is that happening now?

Usually when you talk about being in a valley, you are down in the valley, you are far from the place of conquering on a mountain top.

This is the down position, being in the valley, you have heard about the valley of despair.

Well in Gods timetable in history, He created a whole new valley experience when His people were situated down in the valley in the place of certain defeat, where in the natural you could see that the situation was hopeless.

The first battle involves King Jehoshaphat and the people of God in Judah in the city of Jerusalem. The people of God were facing an enormous army of various opposing mighty nations surrounding them on all sides.

What do you do when you are looking square at the face of defeat? You seek the Lord and submit to His ways and wisdom and rely on His Mighty Arm to save.

The word of the Lord came through the prophet Zechariah.

Zechariah the prophet declared to King Jehoshaphat and the people, 2 Chronicles 20:15 - And he said, "Listen, all you of Judah and you inhabitants of Jerusalem, and you, King Jehoshaphat! Thus says the Lord to you: 'Do not be afraid nor dismayed because of this great multitude, for the battle is not yours, but God's'."

Then we read about prospering when you listen to the Lord and His prophets and follow His instruction.

2 Chronicles:20

20 So they rose early in the morning and went out into the Wilderness of Tekoa; and as they went out, Jehoshaphat stood and said, "Hear me, O Judah and you inhabitants of Jerusalem: Believe in the Lord your God, and you shall be established; believe His prophets, and you shall prosper."

21 And when he had consulted with the people, he appointed those who should sing to the Lord, and who should praise the beauty of holiness, as they went out before the army and were saying: "Praise the Lord, For His mercy endures forever."

22 Now when they began to sing and to praise, the Lord set ambushes against the people of Ammon, Moab, and Mount Seir, who had come against Judah; and they were defeated.

23 For the people of Ammon and Moab stood up against the inhabitants of Mount Seir to utterly kill and destroy them. And when they had made an end of the inhabitants of Seir, they helped to destroy one another.

Praise is a weapon, a spiritual weapon that takes our eyes off the situation and puts our focus on God.

Now the place where they were defeated was in a valley and this valley was renamed as it was a valley of defeat that was transformed into a Valley of Blessing for the people of God. The word Barachah means blessing when translated into English.

The Valley of Berachah.

2 Chronicles:25-30

25 When Jehoshaphat and his people came to take away their spoil, they found among them an abundance of valuables on the dead bodies, and precious jewelry, which they stripped off for themselves, more than they could carry away; and they were three days gathering the spoil because there was so much.

26 And on the fourth day they assembled in the Valley of Berachah, for there they blessed the Lord; therefore the name of that place was called The Valley of Berachah until this day.

27 Then they returned, every man of Judah and Jerusalem, with Jehoshaphat in front of them, to go back to Jerusalem with joy, for the Lord had made them rejoice over their enemies.

28 So they came to Jerusalem, with stringed instruments and harps and trumpets, to the house of the Lord.

29 And the fear of God was on all the kingdoms of those countries when they heard that the Lord had fought against the enemies of Israel.

30 Then the realm of Jehoshaphat was quiet, for his God gave him rest all around.

As you can see this was an enormous turnaround and a suddenly moment for the people of God.

Then how about Abraham, he was a 100 years old and was promised that he would have a son with Sarah his wife who was 99 years old. Against all hope he believed the promise of God and his faith was strengthened and he believed in the God who calls things that appear to be dead and hopeless to be alive.

Romans 4

16 Therefore it is of faith that it might be according to grace, so that the promise might be sure to all the seed, not only to those who are of the law, but also to those who are of the faith of Abraham, who is the father of us all

17 (as it is written, "I have made you a father of many nations") in the presence of Him whom he believed—God, who gives life to the dead and calls those things which do not exist as though they did;

18 who, contrary to hope, in hope believed, so that he became the father of many nations, according to what was spoken, "So shall your descendants be."

19 And not being weak in faith, he did not consider his own body, already dead (since he was about a hundred years old), and the deadness of Sarah's womb.

20 He did not waver at the promise of God through unbelief, but was strengthened in faith, giving glory to God,

21 and being fully convinced that what He had promised He was also able to perform.

[22] *And therefore "it was accounted to him for righteousness."*
We need to apply the faith examples in the impossible situations that we face today. We can be encouraged and strengthen our resolve in these troubled times of uncertainty and confusion where there is a big black cloud of bad news, disinformation psyops, AI created propaganda, lies spread like a virus in the midst of corruption, suppression of free speech platforms, plots to destroy our businesses and incomes, false flag operations, anti-constitutional global dark powers and foreign entities invasion aided by traitors with agendas, infiltration of our Governments, Judiciary and Security Forces; which is an outright attack on us the peoples liberties and freedoms.

Abraham is our example to exercise faith and he is the father of faith. Abraham did not waver but strengthened himself in the Lord, increasing his faith, fully convinced that what God promise He will perform.
What is God saying for our now? What is the promise for His own?

Seek Him, pray and declare His will be done and His Kingdom come in other words come into agreement with God and enter into His rest, which also means standing firm, fighting the fight of faith with the armour of God, this is the reliance on His strength and His ways to defeat the enemies.
Not by might, not by power but by My Spirit says the Lord this mountain will be removed.

Jesus told us to be as wise as serpents and gentle as doves in a crooked world.
Don't riot, don't do anything violent with knee jerk reaction and don't get sucked into being part of the scheme of false flag operations to accuse conservative voices and those wanting justice done with hate crimes to introduce more oppressive laws to control. Don't do anything that opposes the rule of law.

Don't be distracted by all of the noise and media bombardment. Ask for discernment, do your own research, wait on God, ask for His direction and wisdom for what to do and how to combat. God has a strategy that will defeat the enemy every time.
Remember our fight is against spiritual forces in the heavenly realms, 2nd heaven warfare, win the battle here first under the Authority given to us as believers in submission to God.
No it isn't a bunch of higher order origin DNA alien watchers that are coming to rescue mankind either. Aliens equals higher order beings, think the 2nd heaven powers of darkness master deceivers and refer to the Book of Enoch, Nimrod and the tower of babel. Whatever you do, don't get the so called superior Human 2.0 DNA alteration it is a death trap, could mean marked forever.

God reigns above all powers and authorities. Jesus is the King of kings and every knee will bow to Him.

The truth will set you free, the truth will always reign supreme above the lies of this worlds systems of control.

God can do immeasurably more than we hope or imagine.

So what will happen? Something far greater than we could ever possibly imagine, the best plan ever.

Something will go down. Something will shift, shaking, binding the strongman of the deep.

We are rising above the valleys of darkness and defeat into our valley of the blessings of God.

This is a continuation from the last post entitled *"The Valley of Berachah Experience"*.

The God who calls things that do not exist as though they did.

What is that? This is that Faith Talk.

This is faith in action before manifestation. This the engine and the energy of faith.

Energy is not something you can see but it has an effect on things you can see.

Notice God calls things that don't exist into existence.

Now He has delegated believers to be His voice on earth to what He has already established in Heaven.

We are Co-Heirs with Jesus as Jesus is Lord and the Head to the Body of Christ, so let's partner with Him and give voice to what He has said is done in Heaven.

Let's not be detached from Him and speak things that are contrary to His will being done.

Pilate asked Jesus *"what is truth?"* when Jesus was being judged by Pilate the Roman Governor and Pilate went with the crowd and allowed Jesus to be crucified.

People don't always know the truth or see the truth when it is standing right in front of them. Things can't get much worse than that in the natural when you are crucified and you end up six feet under or in Jesus case dead in a tomb. However as we know God always had a plan and was totally in control of the situation.

Faith in action, the promises from the Word of God were announced by the prophets which already declared that Jesus the Messiah would come and save mankind.

Things looked dire to the disciples of Jesus when Jesus was in the tomb those three days and nights.

The disciples were in panic mode at this stage, they had given up on the dream and went fishing.

To make matters worse one of the disciples closest to Him betrayed Him, others denied Him and the rest scattered.

The God who calls things that do not exist as though they did.

Jesus was resurrected and He is the way the truth and the life.

That means no one but Jesus can save us.

The truth is what God says is established in Heaven.

Things on earth need to come into alignment and agreement with Gods will being done and His Kingdom established.

Conversely the lie is whatever is contrary or in opposition to Gods will being done.
We don't want to be on that side of things, that is the darkness.
Have the faith of God, which is the God kind of faith.
See things as He sees them already done and established in Heaven.
Call things that do not exist as though they did.

Are you on the winning team, running the race to win like it is already done?
Are you in agreement with the truth?
We are bombarded by lies and what is truth is being suppressed.
We don't give up because the truth is King and the lies will be exposed and justice will have the final say.
Our Father in Heaven loves His children who are learning the faith language and growing up representing Heavens decrees. Thy will be done on earth as it is in Heaven. Let your Kingdom come.
It's happening people.

God is not panicking or worried about the outcome. Don't worry let the Peace of God rule in your hearts and minds.

Move into your designated sphere of influence, this is delegated authority from God for all believers.
The signs and wonders will follow as we move into agreement with Him.

Chapter 14

300

Looks like I am part of Gideon's 300.
Are you there as well or when the heat is on and
the popular position is stated, why don't you
just accept it?

The Midianites are just too strong, they have
infiltrated our country and we just have to live
with that and pay tribute to their commander
and chief!
Then there is the 300 crazy guys!
These lap dogs are seeing things going on in the
shadows.
So they are telling these 300 crazy people, just
be like the rest of us, bend the knee, drink up
and don't look about you to see what's coming
for you, just accept what is in front of you, this
is reality right!
Wrong!

Not in Gods world!
God doesn't operate like men, His ways are
higher than our ways, He is above our
understanding and He rules over and outside
the restriction of timelines.
So what will happen now?

Man makes all his moves, then God makes His
move, check mate game over! Wait and see when
God plays His unbeatable hand - guess what
Trumped!

So what happens when they only got 300 against a multitude of armies, not just the Midianites but also other enemy nations?

Here is the account of what was against the people of God from *Judges 7* - *"The Midianites and Amalekites, all the people of the East, were lying in the valley as numerous as locusts; and their camels were without number, as the sand by the seashore in multitude."*
This is an army from hell sent against the people of God who have been given the promises of God.
Imagine what was being said in the enemy camp, the bragging and prideful mocking how great they are and how they are the mighty force in control.

Opposition is not a problem for God.
Would be like a bunch of angry soldier ants on a mound against a F22A Fighter Jet.
However from our human perspective if we were part of the 300 we would have good reason to be worried, unless we are convinced that God has given us the strategy and will fight the battle for us.
So God reassured Gideon with insight into what the enemy is thinking through a dream given to the enemy.

Dreams are powerful as they place an impression on top of our thoughts, that influence how we see the world and what will happen.

The final strategy was *"the 300 surrounded the armies at a strategic vantage point above the valley where theses armies were gathered and all blew trumpets and had their lamps lighting up the night sky."*
Without a supernatural intervention this plan would be madness.
Guess what God is into performing what He said He would do and it is miraculous.
The armies who were sleeping in the darkness were all thrown into confusion by God as they awoke to the sound of the the trump and seeing the flashes of light surrounding them.
They went from a position of overwhelming victory to annihilation in one sudden epic moment that changed history.
The timeline of the inevitable was interrupted by God to be completely over thrown, reversed and the will of God was established on earth as it is already done in Heaven.

One moment in time from God can change everything. Trumped!

What comes next after the defeat of the oppressive enemies who oppose the plans and purposes of God?
Restitution.
Restoration of the blessings of God for the Nation.

Remember why has God blessed us?
We have been freely given good things so we can also freely give to others, you need blessings in your hands to hand out blessings to others.

Our Heavenly Father gives us good gifts for our benefit and enjoyment as well as to allow us to be a blessing to others as His children demonstrating the heart of the Father.
It is about the great commission, making disciples of all Nations.
That is also showing compassion to those in need.
Those who call on the Lord will be saved and are qualified for blessing.
Also those who have no voice like the unborn, the oppressed and the enslaved by the corrupt systems of the world.

Immediately after the great armies were defeated by the Glory of God, Gideon called upon all of the people of God to take back what was lost.
Then we see that two enemy princes were captured and killed.

This is significant, who were these two princes and what did they represent?
Now we know that these Old Testament events were given for instruction and it is a spiritual application that we apply. Therefore, death of enemies is a spiritual application, we apply spiritually the killing off of spiritual forces empowering people to do evil things and the head or authority of these powers which are spiritual forces is removed.

Yes these wicked beings operate through people who have been taken captive to do their evil works.

The people who have become leaders and are empowered by dark forces will display in their personalities the characteristics of these evil powers.

Oreb is associated with the creature character of a raven or a crow and also has a reference to a place of influence like a rock being a fortress.

The rock is a strong immovable fortress as well as a mind-set that holds peoples thinking captive under its sway. The Raven is associated with loss or a bad omen, as well as being a talking or prophetic symbol of psychopomps, that are able to transfer messages from the spirit world to the material world.

Zeeb is associated with the character of a wolf with the place of influence being a winepress.

If your nation is ruled by these powers you would be under the influence of the voices from dark spirits overshadowing the thinking of people in its power with a web of menacing lies.

Then there is the other ruling prince that has power over a nation.

The winepress is where pressure is applied creating an intoxicating addictive substance released to bring people under its effects to endure the pressures.

Like being lulled into accepting defeat with false comfort, like fatalistic thinking, you just have to accept defeat and live with it, this is what is meant to be.

The character of this prince is a wolf. Wolf in sheep's clothing comes to mind, has the appearance of being someone on your side, but in reality under this deception is a raiding wild dog sent to deceive and to devour.

Notice that there are two powers at work, not just one leader at work here.

You can make your own conclusions here to what is going on and what fits the descriptions of the raven and the wolf.

The places described as a rock and a winepress are ruling governmental organisations and entities employing many rulers, agents and operatives working their agendas.

Ezekiel 22:27
Her princes within her are like wolves tearing the prey, by shedding blood and destroying lives in order to get dishonest gain.

Isaiah 3:14
The Lord enters into judgment with the elders and princes of His people,
"It is you who have devoured the vineyard;
The plunder of the poor is in your houses.

This is also referencing what I believe is two operations to achieve the agenda.

One governs the people and the other has power over what people believe is the reality.

One is compared to a rock and what does the rock represent - rock solid reliable truth, however if the rock is a counterfeit or hijacked then it is like lies spun as truth, it is something projected as solid that will gain the trust of its citizens.

This persuasion has got people on side convincing them it is truth.
Notice this prince is captured by the armies of Gideon and the head of this prince is taken off. This will mean removed from rule or from the office or position held and therefore will be replaced with truth, righteousness and justice replacing the lies that have held the people captive in a strong delusion.

We know that the solid rock that Jesus refers to is the revelation that Jesus is our Lord and Saviour and He is the Way the Truth and Life and there is none other.

Anyone who is in submission to our Lord is a representative.
Those commissioned by Him have a calling and a purpose and are given authority to rule.

Remember the raven moves in the power and speaks oracles from evil spirits to deceive people. The wolf is the great pretender, he or she pretends to be for the people and doing what is good for the people, but the reality is the Midianites were raiders taking from the people their resources, in other words sending them broke.

In addition to this article about Gideon's 300 and how it is the spiritual application for where things are at and where things are going to, I will conclude with a dream I received on 25th Jan 2021.

I heard someone saying *"I wasn't aware of this Constitution 111 which is able to stop Government!"* It was happening during a major event and like a major news release.

They seem to be a political representative possibly a Senator and was in shock that this power was available to stop the Government under what I assume is safeguard laws of the constitution.
This is what I heard in the dream -
Constitution III - I knew it related to the USA.

After conducting research into the downloaded dream content with some amazement, I found the following legislation regarding
Constitution III.
Constitution Article III Section 3 -
relating to treason against the United States.

I am not sure what the legal exact meanings are of this constitution other than protection and judgement of treason.

Yours to decide, weigh up and measure, only do so with the guidance of the Holy Spirit who leads us into all truth and shows us things to come.

God only knows the exact details of the outcomes and the legal implications of how and when this will be applied, I believe it is already applied in the Heavenly Courts and I heard *"Trump will have his day in court".*

Chapter 15

Symbolic Race the Americas Cup

How about this one people, patriots? Those who are asking hard questions, those wanting answers and those who are not sure, confused, flipping one way then another.

The Americas Cup was traditionally dominated by USA since its beginnings in 1851
until recently when firstly Australia won it dramatically for the first time in 1983.
Now New Zealand have got into the act and are the reigning champs of this prestigious yacht race.
Notice how New Zealand have been praised for handling the COVID Pandemic and are the model Nation for others to follow.
This has been the challenge for western countries managing this pandemic which is debatable whether it is a genuine pandemic or is it a Positive PCR done over 24 Cycles Test pandemic? *(reader do some research on recommended 24 cycles increased to 40 cycles used for the PCR Test)*

Question is while managing the pandemic what is the effect on western economies and is there certain nations and some in the elite billionaire class that are benefiting from this economic hit while the rest suffer?

Now looking at the most recent race on the 30th Jan 2021 in New Zealand we have USA v Italy.

In the races leading up to this concluding race the American yacht had been plagued with technical issues from day one where it sped to the lead as expected but then suddenly the boat flipped over on the turn in the first race and from there it was game over.

Does this sound familiar? November 3rd a certain event happened where results flipped over causing the other challenger to win. Since then the America Yacht has been crippled and unable to get back in the lead.

Now to top off this result we have the final race where America had to win to keep its chances alive on the 30th Jan. In the first race on this day USA came pretty close with no mishaps but still not enough to pass the challenger.

Then came this final race where this could have been declared a draw keeping hopes alive if America won sending things into the tie breaker with extra races to name a winner.

What happened however was a major hit to the yachts remaining hopes, this time there was a bug in the computer system disabling the yachts abilities and it lost the race convincingly unable to regain control due to this major technical hitch in the system.

This is a symbolic event with a reference to the actual event.

Not saying the Italian crew somehow disabled
the American yacht and the result will be turned
by the judges, no that one is done all above
board and happened symbolically to point to an
actual event where things were dodgy.

If we research the real news. it happens that
Italy did it! and all roads lead to Rome, as in the
American Embassy in Rome where a collusion of
countries with an agenda had Operatives with
highly specialised computer manipulation
capabilities switched a ton of data from the
already questionable Voting Software Systems
which are connected to the internet through a
back door by using military grade encryption
with the Leonardo satellite system to cover up
this major manipulation, turned the result
around, flipped it, draw your own conclusions.

Join the dots, see the connections, no joke it
happened, what do you think will happen now?
Justice will strike the hammer blow!

Chapter 16

Twelve Year Old Miracle

You know how things should have gone down.
This is what was meant to happen.
But when the time came, the moment when all
was supposed to happen.
Nothing did happen as we supposed and then
the let-down.
Discouragement supreme and that means all of
the doubters and sceptics were right.
They calculated, they did the sums it doesn't
add up, there might be a discrepancy but it is all
over now, the experts speculated, checked all of
the legal options, lets reason this outcome need
to keep our mouths shut tow the line, do not
dispute this accept it and move on.

The girl died so do not bother the Master any
longer it's just too late!
In other words don't bother God anymore, it's
too late He can't do anything now.
Jesus was moving and a great crowd
encompassed Him about as they followed Him to
see what amazing miracles He will do, they have
seen the signs and wonders, heard Him speak
with Authority, even the demons were subject to
Him, they have never seen anything like this
before in Israel, is He truly the Messiah?
Now Jarius who was a Synagogue Ruler
approached Him and pleaded with Jesus to
come and heal his daughter who was sick and
dying.

Jesus saw his plea and his heart crying for help, Jesus was moved with compassion and was on His way to the girl to heal her.
You can read the full account in Mark 5.

Now there was a woman who suffered greatly from an issue of blood and this condition took her strength away and also caused her shame of being unclean to the public as well as robbing her finances as she spent it all on the physicians to help her but nothing improved.
This woman was desperate but she found faith in her heart and said, *"if I just touch the hem of Jesus garment I will be healed."*
Well this poor woman had this condition for 12 long years.

With faith rising she found the courage to get close to Jesus, but there was a problem, she had to go out in public, she was sick, considered unclean, so the need for social distancing.
But she was determined, she knows what she believes in her heart, so she had to work against the crowd pushing and shoving all around Jesus, she just had to keep moving despite the shame of being considered unclean in public places.

There was no way she could exercise social distancing in her desperation and the only way was to go through the crowd to get close enough to Jesus to meet her expectations in faith.
The moment came and as she touched His garment the miracle happened and she was healed instantly.

Jesus felt the healing power leave Him to heal her and then called her out as she thought I will just slip away and nobody needs to know about this.

But now, *"oh no I have broken the law, I should have just stayed home and lived with it"*; but Jesus wasn't there to tell her off for her audacious faith, no He commended her, *"well done your faith has made you well"*.

Take note the crowd and popular thinking, this is what pleases the Lord.

This woman found healing and was now in peace and the story continues as Jesus is informed the sick girl is now dead and it is now too late.

Let's look at this symbolically and apply these faith principles to a now perspective.

Suppose that this woman represents the church which has been in desperate need of revival for some time now, but has this issue that keeps her in a confined place.

The prophetic within the church has seen it, they have prophesied it, they have tasted it and they know it is coming, there is a wave coming on the horizon.

Revivals like when the glory of God comes in like Azusa Street, the Welsh Revival, the Hebrides Revival, Argentina to name a few.

There are some in the Body of Christ that have been in intercession for what seems like a lifetime, waiting on God to come again and while we know that God is here and His promises are Yes and Amen, we are just aren't seeing it happen to the degree like in the vision.

We know that deep down there is more than what we have experienced other than pockets here and there, we know that we can have the greater works, the Glory is filling the earth and nations are being transformed, it is a done deal until we look outside and see the news.

Hope deferred the heart is getting sick, we are bleeding and we don't want to go out just now, yes we still do what we can but we have lost that zing.

This is especially for those that can relate to this in some way, you haven't arrived yet, it's on the horizon, but there is this oppressive resistance and lots of bad news internally and externally, you still have the faith, you got the flicker of the flame but you know there is so much more. Have you ever been discouraged?

This is also about public perception of Christianity and the Church overall, shame from the failures and no longer seen as the relevant mover and shaker, just some same old narrow minded old Sunday School fairy-tale believers doing their thing.

We got some dazzling light shows on Sunday and some smoke and then a bit of a pep talk on Sunday, but really is the Christian faith on the way out now? In 2020 Covid and lockdowns have shut it down, we have got the virus now and we are being erased from the history books, hit with the cancel stamp, frowned upon and rejected by the educators and popular social network thinking as non-accepting of cultures and judgmental, the church is now viewed as no longer applicable just a sick old lady with bleeding issues bashing people with the bible.

The financial and ruling systems and the so called techno experts of this world have doctored with the church, stealing all of her resources and offering bad advice under the guise of making her well and becoming absorbed by the infiltrating brave new world socially acceptable global community philosophies, but her condition only got worse, still considered unclean and rejected especially in the eyes of the popular cultures.

All is not lost, the world is good at creating their preferred narratives which is a delusion.Think about what the number 12 represents, there were 12 disciples like church Government, 12 months which is to do with a completion of a time period, Jarius was a ruler of a temple, think about that, we are the temple of God, the cornerstone is Jesus, we are the stones that make up the body, this ruler like any father loves her daughter and will do anything to see her live and complete the journey.

When we add the element of completion of time it is already ordained to be fulfilled. There are two instances of 12, the woman who is the church and the girl who is the birthing of the end time harvest of souls, so this is a double portion emphasis, one overlay on top of another in the layers of a prophetically declared timeline.

Bring all of these dynamics into the now and you will see a picture emerging, it is on the horizon and faith is bringing into existence what is unseen and superimposing it into the timeline of the now, where it is already destined to be so.

OK so let's apply this into our now, 12 years ago was 2009, Obama was newly elected and served 8 years, next Trump came to office but then the virus came and this is really sick and now what he is gone, that should not have happened. More bad news.

Let's look at it this way, symbolically 12 years ago and perhaps it was about this time that it was becoming obvious that the church was afflicted, revival was meant to happen and we were going to shake the world on a grand scale, however in the first 4 years things got steadily worse, followed by four more years really going downhill, after that gained some ground and we were starting to fight back, but not really getting the ascendency like in the vision.

Still we are hanging on until finally we just know that if we don't keep contending for the faith and the coming Glory of God all is lost.

Now the precious revival child died, she didn't make it to maturity and got really sick and suddenly when we were waiting for Jesus to show the girl died. What is the little girl, the birthing of our destiny, the vision and what we can see in the spirit which is the coming great end time revival?

But the news is saying Trump is gone, the vote is in and they have decided, do not bother God anymore it's all over He can't do anything now. We can connect this event as well to the girl dying.
The girl hasn't yet even reached maturity and she is now dead.

How then can we compare the moment when we touched the hem of His garment and His healing virtue went through our entire body?

We came alive, filled with the Glory of God, Christ in us is the hope of Glory, we have mounted up on wings of the eagle, we have His compassion and the life of God is motivating us and we have what the world needs now.

This is the moment when we get so close to Jesus, we can reach out and touch Him, His presence is all around us as we have pushed through all of the odds coming against us and the negativity of being viewed as a loser on the world stage.

This is *Psalm 91* in action, we are dwelling under the shadow of the Almighty, we are in the secret place, we are so close to Him and His heart that we are following Him in faith to raise up that girl, going where He is going in compassion we have His healing virtue, nothing can stop us now.

That's what I am seeing.
The End Time Harvest is here, it is resurrected, it is starting to happen and is beginning to break out into our timeline.
Think about a twelve year old and how much longer they will live, growing up reaching maturity they have a lot of living to do, that is the picture that I have here.

The woman pushed through the crowd with the odds stacked against her, in faith she got revived and then Jesus kept going on His way to the girl called revival and raised her from the dead.
Revival got really sick in 2020, with Covid 19 and all of the restrictions, pretty much laid up the church at home and then 2021 came and Trump no longer held office.

Is revival and Trump connected?
They are not the same, but is there a connection!
Can revival happen in a socialist run country?
Yes it can, just look at the totalitarian governments to see how that goes for our freedoms.

The mind control programming camps for those who don't conform, churches demolished, meetings outlawed, bibles smuggled then hidden from view that's just how it is.
Great when your kids are programmed by the state education system in the cancel culture doctrines and the corrupted philosophies of the world after injecting them with a DNA altering jab.

Can revival happen when the church is persecuted by the Government? Yes it can, that's already happened in most Western countries and we see the evidence of this during the Covid lockdowns.
So we will just carry on that way shall we, we will just have to bend the knee to our oppressors!

So God promises us an outcome and then a month later, oh no didn't see that coming, conditional sorry, I got your hopes up, pay attention to the sceptics now.

From what I have heard our dear brothers and sisters in Christ, Millions of Chinese Christians are praying and they are still praying for Trump.

Proverbs 29:2
When the righteous increase, the people rejoice,
But when a wicked man rules, people groan.
Proverbs 28:15
Like a roaring lion and a rushing bear
Is a wicked ruler over a poor people.

Isaiah 10:1
Woe to those who enact evil statutes
And to those who constantly record unjust
decisions,
Micah 7:3
Concerning evil, both hands do it well.
The prince asks, also the judge, for a bribe,
And a great man speaks the desire of his soul;
So they weave it together.
Isaiah 1:23
Your rulers are rebels
And companions of thieves;
Everyone loves a bribe
And chases after rewards.
They do not defend the orphan,
Nor does the widow's plea come before them.

Are you telling me this kind of corruption isn't happening? Or are we supposed to carry on regardless and tolerate it?

Just what I am seeing here, you might say no don't worry about it God is in control, just how it is let the socialism come it is still a democracy, Christianity outlawed, abortions running non-stop, country overrun by violence, laws to protect businesses and families are dashed, end of the middle class it is cancelled, enterprise and self-sufficiency burnt down and we will all line up for our weekly allowance while the billionaire globalist companies rake in the money and gain more control.

What did God say to Adam and Eve have
dominion, that is not tolerate it is dominate, that
isn't *"Que Sera, Sera (Whatever Will Be, Will Be)"*
the world will have dominion over you.

There are principalities and dominions and the
ruler of this world is running amuck with lies,
stealing and killing, just getting their way
unopposed, but you don't have to think about
that until it is on your doorstep and all of your
rights and defences have been taken off you.

Dominion I think they have something to do with
the voting but that's just how it is.

After all we just have to bend the knee, *the
future is not ours to see!* Stick our heads into the
sand, see no evil, hear no evil.

Not so! The Holy Spirit leads us into all truth
and shows us things to come. He warns us so
that we can do something about it!

We are not conforming to the pattern of this
world, our minds are renewed and we can
operate in the perfect will of God.

The Saints of God have the fire of God burning
brightly, their spirits are alive and they won't
back down to the system of this world.

They are praying, seeking, asking and knocking, they have appealed to Heaven and their prayers are a pleasant incense that have been answered in the courts of Heaven and the response will find its way into the earth realm like a lightning bolt and a hammer blow, boom, all fall down, because greater is He that is in His representatives doing His will and exercising His Authority right here where we are told have dominion.

Where is that in the Word of God?
Zechariah 1
18 Then I looked up, and there before me were four horns.
19 I asked the angel who was speaking to me, "What are these?"
He answered me, "These are the horns that scattered Judah, Israel and Jerusalem."
20 Then the Lord showed me four craftsmen.
21 I asked, "What are these coming to do?"
He answered, "These are the horns that scattered Judah so that no one could raise their head, but the craftsmen have come to terrify them and throw down these horns of the nations who lifted up their horns against the land of Judah to scatter its people."

Isaiah 10
27 And it shall come to pass in that day, that his burden shall be taken away from off thy shoulder, and his yoke from off thy neck, and the yoke shall be destroyed because of the anointing.

Psalm 149
Praise the Lord!
Sing to the Lord a new song,
And His praise in the assembly of saints.
2 Let Israel rejoice in their Maker;
Let the children of Zion be joyful in their King.
3 Let them praise His name with the dance;
Let them sing praises to Him with the timbrel and harp.
4 For the Lord takes pleasure in His people;
He will beautify the humble with salvation.
5 Let the saints be joyful in glory;
Let them sing aloud on their beds.
6 Let the high praises of God be in their mouth,
And a two-edged sword in their hand,
7 To execute vengeance on the nations,
And punishments on the peoples;
8 To bind their kings with chains,
And their nobles with fetters of iron;
9 To execute on them the written judgment—
This honor have all His saints.
Praise the Lord!

We apply this as a spiritual battle against the rulers and authorities *(the gods)* in the second heavens and then this will cause those leaders empowered by these forces to crumble, the church is repenting and being conformed into Christs image, nations will be changed, corruption exposed, justice will come, whole lot of shaking going on right now!

I suggest we get with God's program, stop yielding to the programs of men and exercise our God given Authority here on earth.

Have the God kind of faith and those mountains will move.

Some of the things mentioned here are confirmed by what other prophets are saying, these mighty men and women of God come from all over the globe and are not swayed by the main media news or others opinions.

Yes weigh it up, weigh up the words, do your research, pray it through, this a a good thing and should be welcomed that you blindly don't accept everything you see or hear as truth, we won't cancel you for disagreeing, rather we pray for the Body of Christ to be of the same Mind.

Sceptics and doubters are the ones who have made their mind up and they feel like they are the appointed policeman for God shooting down any offenders.

Its Ok to have some doubts, questions, dealing with confusion, needing confirmation, that is the healthy journey, as well as pointing out errors in love, we see in part and are learning more, seeing more, growing up in Him.

Look in the bible, God asked the men of faith to do some pretty outlandish things with no hope in sight like a 100 year old having a baby, marching around blowing trumpets for seven days to make the walls come down, if you were around then it would look pretty crazy, these crazy faith people.

Contend for the faith entrusted to the Body of Christ, love Him and others and occupy until He returns.

Chapter 17

Do the Maths!

Dedicated Sniper.

We all have specific calls and assignments that have been appointed for each one of us and these match our specific talents, gifts and personality. We are His workmanship appointed for good works that He has already planned for us or predestined for us to be and do by His grace giftings and measure of faith apportioned to fulfil our call. Best News is that it is a delight even though there are trials because we fit like a glove our specific call, all things work out for good for those who love God and are called according to His purpose.

Consider the Sniper, in the service of an army against a hostile enemy, the sniper is specifically given assignments and has a specific target, he studies the enemy knows his movements' habits and positions himself to take out the target. One such sniper in a war took out a General, that was his mission and what an effect that had. *(We are talking about a spiritual war how this applied not targeting people but the spirits, powers working through people - I had to add this as it can be misrepresented - our battle is not against people using human earthly weapons - we are talking about spiritual weapons to take down strongholds - prayer, decrees, praise, blowing trumpets or however God directs you, usually different each time a specific strategy just be obedient.*

No lone rangers and wild lone wolves, instead be a warrior for God under His command)

Psalms 2

Why do the heathen rage, and the people imagine a vain thing?

2 The kings of the earth set themselves, and the rulers take counsel together, against the Lord, and against his anointed, saying,

3 Let us break their bands asunder, and cast away their cords from us.

4 He that sitteth in the heavens shall laugh: the Lord shall have them in derision.

5 Then shall he speak unto them in his wrath, and vex them in his sore displeasure.

6 Yet have I set my king upon my holy hill of Zion.

7 I will declare the decree: the Lord hath said unto me, Thou art my Son; this day have I begotten thee.

8 Ask of me, and I shall give thee the heathen for thine inheritance, and the uttermost parts of the earth for thy possession.

9 Thou shalt break them with a rod of iron; thou shalt dash them in pieces like a potter's vessel.

10 Be wise now therefore, O ye kings: be instructed, ye judges of the earth.

11 Serve the Lord with fear, and rejoice with trembling.

12 Kiss the Son, lest he be angry, and ye perish from the way, when his wrath is kindled but a little. Blessed are all they that put their trust in him.

Now the sniper *(I will say he or she just to be sure I mean all are called)* will use stealth and camouflage to remain hidden from the enemy.

In other words he won't announce to the enemy I am coming to get you and this is how I will do it, the sniper is cloaked from the enemy and therefore the enemy doesn't know what's coming.

Matthew 10:16

Behold, I send you forth as sheep in the midst of wolves: be ye therefore wise as serpents, and harmless as doves.

The enemy is usually full of pride and arrogant and his actions will bring him into a downfall, so when we see from Gods vantage point and take action in the timing of the Lord we will hit the target with anointed precision.

The Lord will direct your paths so you will have great success and accomplish earth shaking victories bringing Good News.

The enemy has a plan to enslave the people of the earth in the systems of control which will sooner or later destroy them, God has a plan that overturns the destructions plotted to save us and release a great worldwide harvest of souls.

We are not going down into the pits of darkness and misery, arise shine, the glory of the Lord has arisen in us and will fill the earth with His goodness that sets the captives free.

Some *say "I predict pain, a lot of pain"*, but I *say "I predict signs, wonders and miracles in abundance - your light has come, this little light of mine, we are shining brighter and brighter"*.

Whatever your gift your call, your desires, when you are positioned and operating within your sphere of influence you will make the difference that changes the world into a better place.
The Kingdom of God is advancing and the violent are taking it by force. Faith - Action - mission accomplished. Well Done! Jesus loves you where you are at - waking up - in training - hitting the target.
2 Corinthians 10
13 We, however, will not boast beyond proper limits, but will confine our boasting to the sphere of service God himself has assigned to us, a sphere that also includes you.
Seeing Beyond 2020 Vision we will hit the target every time.

Do the Maths!
The great reset where Billionaires will end up owning everything and we the people will own nothing creating their idea of equality to disempower the people from having independence and empowerment to be who they are created to be having dominion in their appointed sphere of influence.

You will own nothing and be happy what a sucker punch!
God gives us power to create wealth.
Jesus came to give us life and life in abundance.

214

Guess what Satan comes to steal, kill and
destroy.
I got news for you, the elitist corrupted
billionaires owning everything and you owning
nothing is not equality.

Do the maths!
If they really were giving everybody equality then
they would give everyone on the planet including
themselves an equal amount and say go for it
and by the way since we are all equal there is no
totalitarian government control either.
Wake up, having a dictator and the privileged
government party members with higher rank
and control over you is not equality either!
Research into all of the planets wealth shared
equally with the world's total wealth coming it at
$256 trillion would mean we all should get a
share of $34,133.
How does that sound? Like that is real equality!

Do the maths!
Shifting a sum from one side to another making
one side even larger is not equal.
World Dominion Monopoly Oligarchs $Trillions =
$0 us the people.
See that is not equal, sucker punched!
Lies, hypocrisy, contradictions, they are hoping
that we are all stupid.
When they issue propaganda to convince us,
wrap it up in a nice package called equality
sounds like it is a sweet deal.

Do the maths it is a lie.

This is disempowerment of the people and mass control in the hands of the crooked conniving few.

Satan comes to kill steal and destroy.

This sounds like a scheme to rob people, riots and lockdowns destroying businesses is part of the plan to take from the people who have something then conveniently have a fire sale where the billionaires and Totalitarian Governments will buy up transferring ownership.
All part of the agenda which is the people owning nothing.

Robbing the productive innovative enterprising wealth creators to give to the rotten gangster filthy rich.
Kristi Noem, Governor of South Dakota stated something like this: "Covid didn't crush economies, bad actor Government crushed economies and then they printed money like there is no tomorrow for handouts and create economic havoc future debt blowout."

Do the Maths!
The scales are tipped in the favour of the corrupt billionaires and crooked world leaders which is not equal and not fair.

Get a grip, this is not for the people.
The Good News is that there is a day of reckoning where the scales are tipped back to be honest measures.

There is a Kingdom that rules above the kingdoms of this world.

Thy Kingdom come. Thy will be done on earth as it is in Heaven.

Get real, equality is not the answer it just doesn't work that way, if all own a car, you don't give a child a car to drive, you give the children a fair opportunity to own a car when they mature with training and in a proper position to purchase one.

This gives you a clue, when the child matures more responsibility and possessions are given by the Father because they can handle it and not waste it or allow it to destroy them.
So it is with us believers in Christ, we need to mature and become Christ like in order for the Father to promote us and give us more authority to rule and reign.
Need help, draw near to Him and He will draw near to you with grace and mercy to help us become who He said we are in Him, as He is so are we in this world.

Equity is the answer, because it is more individually tailored with fairness for each individual where they are at with what they have been given in talents and abilities.
It's about using your God given talents and abilities with faith to be prosperous, be blessed and make a positive contribution in this world.

That's how God has set things up.

Don't mess with the times and seasons and the laws that God has established.

When Gods Kingdom is activated it will be like a huge hammer that crushes and pounds the pyramid scheme agenda to dust.

Psalm 64
Hear my voice, O God, in my meditation;
Preserve my life from fear of the enemy.
2 Hide me from the secret plots of the wicked,
From the rebellion of the workers of iniquity,
3 Who sharpen their tongue like a sword,
And bend their bows to shoot their arrows—bitter words,
4 That they may shoot in secret at the blameless;
Suddenly they shoot at him and do not fear.
5 They encourage themselves in an evil matter;
They talk of laying snares secretly;
They say, "Who will see them?"
6 They devise iniquities:
"We have perfected a shrewd scheme."
Both the inward thought and the heart of man are deep.
7 But God shall shoot at them with an arrow;
Suddenly they shall be wounded.
8 So He will make them stumble over their own tongue;
All who see them shall flee away.
9 All men shall fear,
And shall declare the work of God;
For they shall wisely consider His doing.
10 The righteous shall be glad in the Lord, and trust in Him.
And all the upright in heart shall glory.

Goodbye reset. Hello recovery, renewal, recompense, and restoration of what was stolen.

Gods Glory is coming and it will fill the earth, people will be set free from the oppression of darkness that covers the earth implemented by the plots and schemes of the corrupt agents for the enemy of Gods perfect plans.
It is time for Gods Agents and Angels to be released bringing change to the current affairs of this world.
Harvest time and reversal from slavery to the liberty of the sons and daughters of God.

OK we have church leaders and Pastors evangelicals who are saying we can't discuss the political election fraud *(alleged)* need to add that word for legal reasons as I am not making the case and am not a legal authority who has examined all of the evidence from both sides.

However, having done sufficient research, critical thinking for myself, not being influenced by the media fabrications and algorithms, asking for wisdom and insight, it was stolen, Mexico knows it, Italy knows it, most know it happened, but zip it they say.

Blind Freddy knows this was rigged, shenanigans went on, there is massive corruption going on and an elitist socialist Marxist global agenda which is opposed to our faith and families.

Opposed to us making a decent income, opposed to businesses wants to burn them down hires the mob, supports abortion which is an abomination against Gods greatest creation made in His own image and they want to tax some extra carbon while certain big countries making the largest contributions get off Scott free and can continue billowing out the smoke thank you very much but that is another subject but related to all owning nothing and being happy, I don't think so as I said earlier do the maths billionaires and global dictators and jobs for the boys own more and you own nothing sucker punched big time!

So everything is dandy, let's just get on with life and let them do their takeover and mass eradication with a jab.
We aren't allowed to pray in schools and soon they will come for our bibles and put our kids in training camps to indoctrinate them into the globalist philosophy of demons.

Getting back to the church leaders in agreement to just how it is, here is a connection and I am not saying it is for sure in all cases, don't have proof but something doesn't smell right in this regard, now there are always the genuinely deceived bunch who won't fall into this, they sincerely believe they are doing the right thing, but as we know being deceived is not a good outcome.

Blind guides leading the blind into a ditch.

No condemnation, we are all deceived and are on a journey to be Christ like, but for the grace of God where would we be?
Where would I be?

Probably with the dark force, so Jesus loves us all and wants us all saved and then thinking renewed from the patterns of this world, it is a growth journey, caterpillar to butterfly and God is still calling all to be of the same mind.

I was in the other camp at one stage, pushed around by the waves of cunning doctrines, lost and blind to what is really going on in the shadows, going along with it, partying, escaping, there is always hope for the worst, look at Saul who persecuted the church killing some, became the greatest Apostle Paul, wrote most of the New Testament, some of you out there could be another Paul.

God save them all, give them a future that you planned before time began.

Ephesians 4:14-16 NIV
[14]Then we will no longer be infants, tossed back and forth by the waves, and blown here and there by every wind of teaching and by the cunning and craftiness of people in their deceitful scheming.
[15] Instead, speaking the truth in love, we will grow to become in every respect the mature body of him who is the head, that is, Christ.

16 From him the whole body, joined and held together by every supporting ligament, grows and builds itself up in love, as each part does its work.

Ok here is the point!

Do some research into this topic, Christian Groups Take Money from Atheist Billionaire George Soros. Follow the money!

Soros contributing funds to Christian Organisations. Is this leverage?
You draw your own conclusions. As I said does not apply to all in this group, but just have that feeling something not right here!!!

Rent an evangelical, they will play any tune - puppet on a string.

Just something to mull over with a strong cup of coffee to wake us up!

Do the Maths!
You can figure this out!
Two plus two equals four more years!

Chapter 18

Rhyme and a Reason

Pop goes the weasel!

The sound of the weasel popping off will be heard loud and clear in and out the eagle, as soon as the monkey stopped to pull up his sock, pop goes the weasel!

The whistle blowers will be popping off, it is happening already and has been intensifying, but now it is headed for Krakatoa, a massive unstoppable historic eruption with worldwide consequences!

Whistle blowers can be a very significant personnel and what they say will not be able to be refuted or denied and swept under the carpet. There are ways and means to get the information simultaneously and continually to the government agencies, authorities, mainstream and alternative media, social media and all of the filters will not be able to stop it!

Once the big one happens, a lot more will come out of the woodwork, popping their head out and they won't be the only ones becoming visible to the public, corruption and lies will be exposed with an unprecedented explosive cloud covering the earth, increasing uncontrollable numbers will surface from their caves with security measures in place for their protection.

If those who should take action don't, they will be exposed, due to the spread of information and it is known if they are not compromised they must take action and follow the rule of the law or they are not fulfilling their duty and oath to serve.

Security will be easier because of the overwhelming numbers no longer controlled by big brother, brother you are history!

Time is up! The alarm will sound! Loud and clear, get your house in order or suffer the consequences and too late to cover up, erase and hide the evidence it has already been uncovered and released.

You might be able to run but you can't hide!

I saw someone significant on their laptop releasing information to the strategic targets using smart technology, when you go to capture them they will no longer be there, gone to Timbuktu.

Pop goes the weasel!

Something triggers them and suddenly they will shift from being quiet conforming on side to coming out and sharing all.

I pray for stealth, cloaking and clouds of covering, angels are dispatched for this operation and security over those who will come out to release significant evidence that will turn it all around and shift the current administration of corruption out of practice.

Intercessors if this registers, go to war!

Can you hear the sound of the Mulberry Trees whistling?

"Pop Goes the Weasel" British version:

Half a pound of tuppenny rice,
Half a pound of treacle.
That's the way the money goes,
Pop! goes the weasel.

Up and down the City road,
In and out the Eagle,
That's the way the money goes,
Pop! goes the weasel.

"Pop Goes the Weasel" American version:

All around the Mulberry Bush,
The monkey chased the weasel.
The monkey stopped to pull up his sock,
Pop! goes the weasel.

Half a pound of tuppenny rice,
Half a pound of treacle.
Mix it up and make it nice,
Pop! goes the weasel.

First Published in 1852.

It's happening brothers and sisters.
Give God all the Praise and Glory, He is
revealing hidden things to His servants and
nothing is too hard for Him to change in a flash!

Are you in agreement? Are you for us or against
us? God is for us!

The knowledge of the Glory of the Lord will cover the earth, nothing can stop the coming billion plus harvest.
Gods heart is none should perish and all should come to the knowledge of salvation and we all got our part as coheirs partnering with Him.

Choose Life!

Hickory, Dickory Dock!

Any idea what time it is?
We have been taught as children to read the time.
Other signs then alert us to that time.
The mouse is running up the clock and we know that something is up when the time approaches.
The Clock strikes one and we have arrived, it is past midnight, or is it high noon?
The mouse is alarmed and runs back down.
The mouse can no longer hide, the mouse was getting up to some things, then when that clock strikes, suddenly bingo down he goes in plain sight to all!

The Hickory is being pounded out, flowing like milk and honey, we had to pound this thing, we didn't leave it alone as we would have no cream.

The Dock with the long taproot. When we tried to pull it out only the top came off, but the deep rooted thing stuck around like a noxious weed.
Well when this one finally gets pulled out, we are going to get our tonic and healing after the nation being stung.

When we were young and free we were taught to
tell the time, we used to hear that sound, could
see the mouse going up and down.

Don't you go believing the lying rhymers now,
they package it well, sweetened up media treats,
just a cheap trick clock, don't buy into it or you
will lose the telling time just right.

Tick tock, tick tock!

Hickory Dickory Dock!
The mouse ran up the clock.
The thief came a lying, stealin, cheatin in the
night.
The clock struck one.
The mouse came down.
Hickory Dickory Clock!
The clock will strike and you can't shift the
times and seasons we are in.
Now the clock will strike two, hence the return of
Trump and Pence.

"Hickory Dickory Dock"

Hickory, dickory, dock,
The mouse ran up the clock.
The clock struck one,
The mouse ran down,
Hickory, dickory, dock

First published in London in about 1744.

227

Today I saw a girl blowing bubbles across the street on the other side, it was so pure joy and like a best blessed day.

The wind was blowing a gust and taking the bubbles right across the street and through the traffic, the busyness of life was forgotten in this moment.

You could see them coming towards you and joy was hitting you big time!

This is the thing, this girl represents telling time taught young and with childlike acceptance just accepted it and that is just how it is, so no use trying to change times and seasons!

Our times are in His hands!

In Him we move and have our being, is allowing Him complete access into our lives and He releases us to be who we really are and the result is full of joy and pleasures bubbling over.

The bubbles blowing in the wind of the Holy Spirit will just be poured out all over the place, the passers-by can't help but notice and take it in.

This girl is a picture of the church with youth renewed, childlike and mature all at the same time in Him.

Freedom Bubbles.

Bubbles will be blown by the wind to cover the earth and all will witness these and if they choose to take notice to stop and see this phenomenon which is a supernatural effect on the natural, they will sense the innocence restored by the mercy of God and the pure blood of Jesus takes effect, shed for all mankind to receive.

The blood of Jesus is untainted by the interference of this world and its corruption of what is pure, where Dr Jekyll experiments on humans with DNA manipulations. Genetically modified human beings where pure creation is perverted from the original design, this alteration is sold to the world to be an upgrade and superior, but it will be judged and proper peer reviewed to be decaying grotesque blobs of dark patches.

Gods ways and His judgement brings true freedom as He is wisdom and knows how we are made undefiled, revealing corrupt practices which is lawlessness, where division, hatred and perversion festers, manufacturing all kinds of deadly viruses and plagues, which is the downfall of men in rebellion and pride to a just God.

Do not believe their twisted and evil reports that are a cleverly marketed lie to convince you that this is the best thing since a slice of bread with future benefits and security.

Trusting in Pharaoh and his magicians will only bring the yoke of slavery from a crooked democratic ruler with policies of death from a twisted harsh taskmaster.

Seek the truth and you will find it.

Thank God it is Easter 2021 at the time of this writing, the message of hope and salvation. Jesus died for us and took our sins and the punishments due and then He rose from the dead, so that we can have new life, if only we believe and give our lives to Him. God is Love.

Habakkuk 2:14 — King James Version (KJV 1900)
14 For the earth shall be filled with the knowledge of the glory of the Lord,
As the waters cover the sea.

1 Corinthians 1
18 For the preaching of the cross is to them that perish foolishness; but unto us which are saved it is the power of God.
19 For it is written, I will destroy the wisdom of the wise, and will bring to nothing the understanding of the prudent.
20 Where is the wise? where is the scribe? where is the disputer of this world? hath not God made foolish the wisdom of this world?
21 For after that in the wisdom of God the world by wisdom knew not God, it pleased God by the foolishness of preaching to save them that believe.
22 For the Jews require a sign, and the Greeks seek after wisdom:
23 But we preach Christ crucified, unto the Jews a stumblingblock, and unto the Greeks foolishness;
24 But unto them which are called, both Jews and Greeks, Christ the power of God, and the wisdom of God.
25 Because the foolishness of God is wiser than men; and the weakness of God is stronger than men.
26 For ye see your calling, brethren, how that not many wise men after the flesh, not many mighty, not many noble, are called:

27 But God hath chosen the foolish things of the world to confound the wise; and God hath chosen the weak things of the world to confound the things which are mighty;
28 And base things of the world, and things which are despised, hath God chosen, yea, and things which are not, to bring to nought things that are:
29 That no flesh should glory in his presence.
30 But of him are ye in Christ Jesus, who of God is made unto us wisdom, and righteousness, and sanctification, and redemption:
31 That, according as it is written, He that glorieth, let him glory in the Lord.

Charismatic celebrities and cunning spin doctors are employed to weave self-righteous thinking and lies covered and sweetened by pretentious values and promises and tales of equality and equity.

They are the blind teachers of falsehood and blind guides leading the blind into the pit of doom. What they say and espouse appears to be valid and are convincing to the ones without discernment to see the underlying dark philosophies that have the agenda to replace God with a false god and make us all a god of our own utopias.

They use the algorithms and filters of mind control to suppress the truth and only present their lies, but these bubbles will burst as they do not have true substance and can hold nothing.

The so called wisdom of this world will be destroyed by the Light of truth exposing all of the dark satanic lies and the so called wisdom that controls our media and airwaves infiltrating the thinking of men and women unaware of the danger and corruption effecting them by taking it in as truth, the wisdom that comes from below is demonic in origin and can't be trusted, it has the power to twist pervert and spin great deception on those who allow these lies to take root in their minds taking them down the pathways of destruction and being useful idiots for the enemy opposing the truth.

Lies, lies and more lies will be exposed on an unprecedented and earth shattering Richter Scale.

The Truth will be revealed.
Justice will be served that will leave no stone unturned, documents, evidence of massive deep state rooted corruption will be revealed and the strong arm of the rule of law will act to bring convictions, indictments, with compensation and damages restored.
Those involved in crimes against humanity and treason who are corrupt members of Government, Judiciary and Media who work for their own pockets and do the bidding for dark entities that have an agenda to control and enslave humanity will be convicted for their crimes and overthrown from their positions of power and influence, swept aside by the shaking and sweeping reforms, swiftly bringing justice with no place to hide!

See how they run, see how they run, three blind mice, three blind mice, the corrupt members of Government, Judiciary and Media, three blind mice, three blind mice, their tales got chopped off, did you ever see such a sight?

If people don't repent of their wicked ways of being instruments to spread and infect others then they will be crushed by the weighty glory of God as they run for cover but finding nowhere to escape the true justice.

God is merciful and waits long for people to turn from their wicked ways, they will be warned by many prophets and servants of God speaking the truth even with signs and wonders to convince them of the undeniable truth.

The Gospel is preached and this is Good News.
Resurrection Sunday is a glorious day, now is the day of salvation.
Just be free to be the real you.
Psalm 16:11
11 Thou wilt shew me the path of life: in thy presence is fulness of joy; at thy right hand there are pleasures for evermore.

"Jack be nimble"

Jack be nimble,
Jack be quick,
Jack jump over
The candlestick.

First published around 1815.

Certain Nursery Rhymes are known to have a dark twist to their seemingly harmless fun story and it is a disturbing thing that these kids' kindergarten stories are presented to children with young tender minds to learn about.
Let's look at Disney, harmless entertainment for the family focus on the kiddies, tune into the Mk Ultra training Program for young aspiring actors.

The Media controls your airwaves, your thoughts and what your children will believe.
It is now overturned, reversed and all that was stolen will be restored to those under this enslavement by the dark entities corrupting the planet, we need to turn our trust in the Lord and not lean on our own devices and the strength and power of Pharaoh and the gods of Egypt.

The tables are turned in the favour of justice, all the lies will be exposed, the thieves will be apprehended and tried and what was stolen will be put back in place.

The thief comes to steal, kill and destroy.
The thief does not enter through the door which is Christ Jesus, He comes through an illegitimate way.
The thief steals what is intended for good and corrupts the gifts to be used for his evil plans.
The sheep do not listen to the voice of the stranger, they follow the Shepherd and know His voice is the truth and the Shepherd loves His own and cares for them.
Jesus came that we might have life and life in abundance.

The candle stick delusion.
This rhyme was written with the intention that the ability to leap over a candlestick is as if like magik that Jack was specially empowered to defy the common laws.

But now as this is the time of a great reset which is not the planned great reset but one that is divinely orchestrated where the powers used by corrupt individuals are overthrown.

Things that seem to gain control and get away with all sorts of atrocities to mankind will be judged and tried and the outcome will be reversed!
They are thieves and robbers coming through the illegal door, gaining power from the dark to pull off their sinister schemes and trick the world that this is how things are done.

Behind the secret closed doors will be ripped open and the world will see into this mess and totally abhor it, no longer be subject to it. Those that involve the dark arts and employ tricks to defy the laws will not be able to get away with it any longer as their candle lit power will be extinguished.

Instead the candle of justice will burn all those depending on their magik to leap over the light unscathed and will instead suffer the consequences from the searing heat of the candle of justice.

The Ports and Hotels getting busted in a clean-up operation. A street sweeper will go through cleaning up the traffik and unblocking the truth all about Evergreen Street. The ever smart will be out smarted and container contents will be tipped up.
Weiner gate laptop withdrawn from sale when the videos leaked out. Islands are shaking, their temples falling down, their candle cooked up spirits coming down in cuffs into town, Johnny and company, Isaac saw you and ran up the street pursued, he never did come back and talked no more.

Running rings eating pizza in the networks, Jack be quick the law is coming, Jack be nimble, the judges will no longer play your tune, Jack got fried by the heat of the candlestick.
I hear a true sound coming out of the Wood, whistles blowing in the wind, it is all coming out now and it will rattle the foundations of DC to New York, New York. Revealing winds are blowing stripping it all bare in Georgia, in the deserts of Arizona, all the way through Highway 62 to sunny California will howl, even in Death Valley the Navajo stand up and take notice.

The spirit of man is the candle of the Lord and God will shine a bright burning light on hidden acts of darkness where corruption will be exposed for all to see, no more flying over the radar undetected you have been inspected, tick tock and found wanting.

What worked in the past cloaked in a sinister cloud will feel the flame and fall from the sky with those leaping into this magik come falling down like crazed meteors burning in spectacular fashion for the world to see.

Jack will be caught up in his web of deceit at the height of his leap, the web that was spun to deceive, where sick things are permitted to operate with a blind eye and looking the other way, no questions were asked by the compromised all the way up to the supreme.

Remember with all of the counterfeit gifts there is the true and so it is with Jack.

The prayers and the righteous decrees of the saints have been heard in the Heavenly Court, justice justice, favour favour, the gavel has fallen overturning the dark modus operandi and now the tables are turned.

The rule of law will be applied and the thief caught and will pay for the damages and this will reverse the devastation and what was previously allowed by corrupt rulers to continue without penalty.

Now is the time for the true iconoclastic to arise, these ones are not lawless, they are operating in the spirit of the law, which is the law of the spirit of life where there is grace and protection by the blood of Jesus in the Passover and they have great freedom to perform leaping signs and wonders that will dazzle the whole earth.

A billion souls plus is at stake and this is the awakening and the reason why this all must be reversed, a reverse of the curse, stars for scars, a unprecedented wealth transfer on the way and can't be stopped, it is a glory freight train full of abundance of blessings and wealth.

The Kingdom of God is advancing full steam ahead.
Nothing can stop it, neither death, nor life, nor angels, nor principalities, nor powers, nor things present, nor things to come, nor height, nor depth, nor any other creature can stop the power of love.

Let's turn this thing around for good, Jack the black is saved and delivered, now he is a new creation the old is passed away, Jack in the white light and Jill are saved and delivered they are new creations and the old is history.

Now Jack is true nimble and Jack is true quick, he is now in the light, the only way he cannot disrupt the light on the candlestick is when he is in sync with the light source.
The candle of man is light of the Lord.
Jesus lights up mankind and He is the light of life.

Harmony and flow will anoint you to move with ease through the challenging and the impossible, you will have the freedom to leap like never before witnessed like an iconoclastic Jack turbo charged.

Jack may have a reputation of a dark pirate running from the law, but underneath this skilful character is an individual breaking the mould, not bound by the status quo of conforming to the pattern of mediocrity and the cookie cut woke, saying the same, thinking like the same old parrot taught what to say and think, not how to think!

There is an attitude and a freedom that does not conform to the ways of the world keeping those earthbound, tied down to the constraints imposed by the globalist laws and doctrines of worldly thinking and rules that are pointless imposed by the police states of irrational government control.
God doesn't want us to be fashioned into programmed DNA robots all thinking and saying the same old spouting nonsense.

Iconoclastic Jack.
Gifts are excelling in favour released.

Jack are the elusive fellows with a kind of out of the box reputation, not fitting in to the contrived new norm and conforming by the rules, a mischief to the authorities, he seems to evade capture and is admired by those who can't get out of this box.

When Jesus came He had this type of reputation and the religious authorities despised Him, He wasn't contained and when He moved and spoke it was pure talent and a delight to behold.

He shook society to the core, challenged the norms and He walked on water, you couldn't keep this man down.
The news reported Him, but He didn't say what they wanted and do what they wanted, He was unpredictable impossible to trap, He was above and beyond, He saw above and beyond any 2020. Jesus was walking and talking freedom.

Jesus was the true iconoclastic and we are conformed into His image, do you think that means we all dress the same, look the same, talk the same, say the same arguments lined up like ducks in a row, clowns with open mouths waiting for our next thinking pill and a jab for our DNA alteration? Think again!
He has created us all unique with gifts and callings set apart from others to contribute something new, complimentary and helps support others, filling up the missing pieces lacking in our society and progressing us into completeness in the image of the Head of this Body of believers, Jesus our Lord and Saviour who is the teacher for free thinkers and liberty. Free your mind!
If the Son sets you free you are free indeed.

Born again and saved, free spirited Jack and Jill are going up the mountain.
Jack won't fall down and he will retain his crown.

A peculiar people, Kings and Priests ruling and reigning.

The real trick is not to focus on the problem,
which is all of the corruption and the evil
practices that is going on in this fallen world.

We need to focus on the solution.
The solution is Jesus Christ came to set us free
from our evil ways and give us a new life.
Jesus is the door into freedom where all things
are possible, be nimble and be quickened.

Christ in us is the hope of Glory.

We are the righteousness of God in Him and we
are a new creation the old has gone and the new
has come.
Harvest time is here for Jack and Jill.

Happy Easter Resurrection Sunday.

Peace on earth.

Chapter 19

Build My House

Haggai 1

2 This is what the Lord Almighty says: "These people say, 'The time has not yet come to rebuild the Lord's house.'"

3 Then the word of the Lord came through the prophet Haggai:

4 "Is it a time for you yourselves to be living in your paneled houses, while this house remains a ruin?"

5 Now this is what the Lord Almighty says: "Give careful thought to your ways.

6 You have planted much, but harvested little. You eat, but never have enough. You drink, but never have your fill. You put on clothes, but are not warm. You earn wages, only to put them in a purse with holes in it."

7 This is what the Lord Almighty says: "Give careful thought to your ways.

8 Go up into the mountains and bring down timber and build my house, so that I may take pleasure in it and be honored," says the Lord.

9 "You expected much, but see, it turned out to be little. What you brought home, I blew away. Why?" declares the Lord Almighty. "Because of my house, which remains a ruin, while each of you is busy with your own house.

10 Therefore, because of you the heavens have withheld their dew and the earth its crops.

11 I called for a drought on the fields and the mountains, on the grain, the new wine, the olive oil and everything else the ground produces, on people and livestock, and on all the labor of your hands."
12 Then Zerubbabel son of Shealtiel, Joshua son of Jozadak, the high priest, and the whole remnant of the people obeyed the voice of the Lord their God and the message of the prophet Haggai, because the Lord their God had sent him. And the people feared the Lord.

Know that we are the Lords living temples on earth, building in us a fortress which is the very representation of who He is and what He stands for on earth as it is in Heaven.
We are each the living stones that make up a different part to play and we need to allow Him to mould us and fit us where we need to be to activate our position in what God is building on this earth.

We are His workmanship, we are created in Christ Jesus to do good works, He planned this before the earth was formed and mankind came into being, He already had it in His imagination the works that you and I would perform for the Kingdom of God.

This is what building a hope and a future is about, God is in the building business here on earth and we are His instruments of Glory, the works are described as the greater works by Jesus and He has commissioned each of us to bring Heaven on earth.

Notice in Haggai that this is how things were that the Temple was not a priority, the people of God were about their own business of survival and securing themselves in the land.

But you see the Good News is when they were made aware that the priority should be being about building Gods house and not their own first that then they would really thrive and not just survive.

The people of God then repented and obeyed the Word of God and the message brought by the prophets and so it is today, we are getting our focus back on track seeking first the Kingdom of God and His righteousness and then all these things will also be added.

When you are thrown into survival mode by the onslaught of the storms in life, that's what you tend to do, you just try to make things work making ends meet and then perhaps you can look at the other things.

We all tend to follow survival mode logic and natural thinking that we naturally do when we are under it and are looking after number one, blocking out the voice of God and not hearing what His prophets are saying in this hour.

But as you may have learnt in the faith of God school, it is all turned upside down and right side up, faith seems to call things that are not as though they are, faith goes about moving the mountains of opposition and then nothing is impossible for those that believe and this is when we shift into operating in Gods economy, we make a withdrawal from the banks of the unseen to bring multiplication to the visible, we no longer do subtraction of the resources like the world offers.

This is the now season where I believe we are at as the people of faith, we are now awakened and have shifted our focus to building the house of God, ushering in the Glory of God which will fill the earth.

In the parable of the seeds told by Jesus in the Gospels it mentions the seeds that were choked by the cares of this world and desire for riches swallowed up the life in the seed so it did not produce.

These were thorns and weeds that crept in and were mixed into the garden which is our hearts and what gets our focus and attention in life, so that eventually as they were not dealt with they took over and choked the life out of the seeds producing good fruit.

Can you identify with this scenario, I can and I believe that is where we have been at and God is dealing with us to remove those things that suck the life out of us and choke the good fruit out of our lives.

When the people of God heard the prophets and the Word of God, they repented and turned their priorities back to God fully so that the good fruit would come, this is the fruit of the great harvest that is coming upon the earth, where the Glory of God will cover the globe and strike nations, shake nations and move nations with the greater works, signs, wonders and miracles an overwhelming glory wave cleansing the earth of contamination.

A Billion Souls plus will enter the Kingdom of God as this wave covers the entire globe and there isn't a devil from hell that can stop it, the gates of corruption, control and manipulation that causes death and destruction will not prevail.

Greater is He that is in us than he that is in the world.

Isaiah 60
Arise, shine; for thy light is come, and the glory of the Lord is risen upon thee.
2 For, behold, the darkness shall cover the earth, and gross darkness the people: but the Lord shall arise upon thee, and his glory shall be seen upon thee.
3 And the Gentiles shall come to thy light, and kings to the brightness of thy rising.

Even though we would be in a time where you would say gross darkness covers the earth and evil people with agendas from devils have afflicted the earth with unprecedented wickedness bringing death.

We see that the light has come and the Glory of God has arisen in us, we are His house where His very presence dwells which is why the Glory comes and the light is shining, we are housing His presence and allowing our gifts to glow due to the light of the Lord activated inside our beings.

When this is manifested in brighter intensity, as we become more like Jesus, full of power, authority and compassion, you know what people notice, then they will rush to the alter repenting from their ways and accept Jesus Christ as their Lord and Saviour.
This is a great awakening, the reformation, the revival that will shake not only the heavens but the whole earth.

Sometimes sadly when it seems the darkness is prevailing and nothing changes but gets much worse on earth, God's saints lose their way due to lack of vision.
Proverbs 29:18
Where there is no vision, the people perish: but he that keepeth the law, happy is he.
Perishing is not living, it isn't life in abundance and that is not what Jesus came to give us which is the abundant life, that means plenty of life for us and a lot left over to help others.
When you are struggling to survive, just getting by and the things get on top of you it is hard to sit down and gather your thoughts and say *"I am here for a reason and Gods far out idea for me and my future is much bigger than just getting by street".*

It is hard to think of others when you are under it you know.

This is where we just need to accept that God is greater and nothing is too difficult for Him, believe He is who He says He is and believe who He says we are, pick up our instruments and get on the Glory building team.

Be part of the bright bunch of builders that get up and make a difference, be part of the answer, get your eyes on the master plans of the solution with the God given ability of a problem solver, no longer focused on all of the problems we are the overcomers.

That's why we need to set aside time to be with God, receive His love and acceptance, get hold of His picture that He has about us ruling and reigning with Him; as we allow Him to share the vision He has for us we will delight to be in the wonders that will pour out on others within our sphere.

What does this also mean? Release from the tyranny from evil dictators and corrupt rulers, think about the crimes against humanity and being set free from the perpetrators.

In so many areas in our so called democracies this is what is happening, poverty, planned plagues made in the lab, we are robbed and pillaged by oppressive regimes with sick agendas, even the unborn is killed and the young abused by the current administrations.

They want MK mind controlled zombies to fill our neighbourhoods and streets yelling and waving their false flags peddling lies using intimidation tactics, then they will loot and destroy if they perceive you are successful and can make it on your own.

What happened to looking after the working class and small business that's gone with the wind and cancelled, so the thugs are sent in after the disarming gun control, they are the tools for the cabal to do their dirty work in bringing us all down to the lowest common denominator, easy to control and made into dependents on the evil new order state.

No it doesn't mean a huge fusion hotch potch of nations either all crammed together in a super city hoping for an idealistic mix! Why don't you just allow nations to have their separate identity and culture and stop trying to make us all into a global city that makes us all synthetic digitised paper dolls in a row from the sick plan and warped thinking making humans into a programmable altered DNA species with robotic machine connected behaviours modified by the technocratic big brother AI beast, while the controllers amass the worlds riches and live in secluded castles with heavy security to keep the mob out that they pretend to endorse and tell you this is equality.
The 2030 whacko plan is a fake utopia based on false promises and pretentious do good lies for policies that if you are sucker enough they hope you buy into it.

The curse goes back many generations and has infected our DNA, bringing with it crooked pathways which leads us into captivity and destruction.

Government that is righteous has values that works for the people, giving all a chance to be their own individual expression on earth and make a difference, we can contribute by being uniquely gifted offering something valuable to others.

We don't want no false unity education.
There is the counterfeit that may look good on the surface with some self righteous pride and arrogance that attempts to replace the truth.
Give me the real deal any day.
Ephesians 4
14 that we should no longer be children, tossed to and fro and carried about with every wind of doctrine, by the trickery of men, in the cunning craftiness of deceitful plotting,
15 but, speaking the truth in love, may grow up in all things into Him who is the head—Christ—
16 from whom the whole body, joined and knit together by what every joint supplies, according to the effective working by which every part does its share, causes growth of the body for the edifying of itself in love.

As Jesus is so are we in this world.
We are anointed and appointed to go forth and produce much good fruit.

The Good News is preached, the broken hearted are healed and the captives are set free.

When the Glory comes we will rebuild the ruins of societies and repair cities to be shining habitations where people's rights and freedoms are not abused by tyrannical maniacs greedy for power and intent on killing us off so they can have the planet all to themselves.
Look out buddy boys the great wealth transfer will happen sooner than you think, knock knock on your door! God will remove the wealth from the wicked and transfer it to those who are about building Gods House.
The main thing is that lives will be transformed and we will be filled by the Spirit of God knowing love, joy and peace.

The main thing is that each one knows God and knows they are accepted and loved by Him with an everlasting love and we will love to spread the Good News to all Nations so that all will come to know Him.

Isaiah 61 "The Spirit of the Lord God is upon Me,
Because the Lord has anointed Me
To preach good tidings to the poor;
He has sent Me to heal the brokenhearted,
To proclaim liberty to the captives,
And the opening of the prison to those who are
bound;
2 To proclaim the acceptable year of the Lord,
And the day of vengeance of our God;
To comfort all who mourn,

3 To console those who mourn in Zion,
To give them beauty for ashes,
The oil of joy for mourning,
The garment of praise for the spirit of heaviness;
That they may be called trees of righteousness,
The planting of the Lord, that He may be
glorified."
4 And they shall rebuild the old ruins,
They shall raise up the former desolations,
And they shall repair the ruined cities,
The desolations of many generations.

With eagle eye precision and divine insight into mysteries of God into the Kingdom Age, the built up temple of believers' vision is being restored. Our eyes are open and we are now Seeing Beyond 2020 Vision.

The Temple of God which is being raised up for this very hour will overwhelm the nations like a tsunami wave flood of righteousness, justice and truth which will clean out the filth of manmade structures and systems of evil control.

What do you see? The Glory of the Temple of God on earth which is built in pure glistening gold is radiating pure glowing light to the nations of this world.

The Gold and Silver are Gods and we are His own.
Be blessed to be a blessing.

Chapter 20

Progressive Faith

That's what it is all about being progressive, advancing forward learning from history and the mistakes of the past to build a better future and a better world for everyone.

The best laid plans by mice and men.
Will we find any faith?
Without faith it is impossible to please God.

What is the source of our forward thinking?

Self ambition, self promotion, self achievement, self discipline, self ideals, self ethics, self agendas.

But also what about collective ambitions collective achievements collective disciplines collective ideals collective ethics collective agendas all for the common good, you say we want a revolution to change society for the better.

Sounds like the plan! The progressive plan to knock them all down.
Thankyou Mr Nobel forward thinking.

Nobel has three meanings, an aristocrat of high rank in society, or someone achieving beneficial things for society and it is awarded as a prize, as well as someone with high morals.

What is the heart motivation behind, *"let's do great things and make our mark on society?"*

History shows that the actors on the classic stage wore masks!

The sword of God's Word goes deep below the surface of things to reveal any ulterior heart motives and whether what is done is in alignment with Gods will being done on earth or is influenced by deceptive doctrines and false beliefs as well as the mask of false humility.

We need discernment to know if these prize seeking nobel gestures have the just an appearance of an outward show of a good act, or are of genuine faith from pure motives.

We all need to come into the faith of God to produce good fruit.

What is healthy for our faith is that we are abiding in Him to allow Him to be the source of our desires and what we do on this earth during our time here to make our own unique mark. It is a good noble thing when we are partaking of the divine nature which develops our faith into bearing good fruit and increasing in the healthy growth on the vine, this will include allowing the pruning of the dead wood away to promote healthier regrowth.

When we examine Pauls prayer in Ephesians there appears a progression into fullness.

I have seen a progression of faith.

Ephesians 3
*15 Of whom the whole family in heaven and earth
is named,*
*16 That he would grant you, according to the
riches of his glory, to be strengthened with might
by his Spirit in the inner man;*
*17 That Christ may dwell in your hearts by faith;
that ye, being rooted and grounded in love,*
*18 May be able to comprehend with all saints
what is the breadth, and length, and depth, and
height;*
*19 And to know the love of Christ, which passeth
knowledge, that ye might be filled with all the
fulness of God.*
*20 Now unto him that is able to do exceeding
abundantly above all that we ask or think,
according to the power that worketh in us,*
*21 Unto him be glory in the church by Christ Jesus
throughout all ages, world without end. Amen.*

When we abide in the vine and God is our
source we are tapped into the might of the Holy
Spirit that inspires our faith.
The more we get to know Him, the more we
reflect His love which passes what we think we
know is love, as if we know better than God
regarding the affairs of the world and how
everyone should live and act.

No Government is meant to take the Fathers role
of governing like gods how we live and act and
the rules that we should obey.

Governments are there to administer justice and laws that are based on Gods principles, they are servants faithfully there for the people and they do deserve our full respect and obedience when they administer faithfully representing the King of kings.
We don't expect perfection from anyone in leadership and many don't even know God, but they still are ruled by a good conscience demonstrating justice and equity.

Yes you should follow the rules you know like you don't go speeding or driving on the wrong side of the road, just follow your God given conscience, the inner man, the inner voice, then if there are laws that are causing offence, then follow His leading how to respond, don't react, respond by faith.

We could mention a law allowing abortion for example.
Does this contradict Gods laws? Killing of the innocents and defenceless.

This is not a condemnation for anyone who felt there was no way out and went through this. There is forgiveness for all who call on the Name of the Lord. This is referring to the illegitimate law makers that promote killing fields of clinics and covertly hold dark occultist masses staining the land with bloodshed and evil.

God's wisdom is above man's wisdom and His ways are higher. Man's wisdom is foolishness to God.

If you see what the devil does, lying, stealing and killing then you know that is evil.

Don't call evil good and good evil that is foolishness and rebellion!!!

We are not all mini gods who are independent beings making up our own contrived mini universes. There are some on this earth now who have accumulated great wealth and power who think they can play god with others' lives, they will be met with the fist of God like a hammer blow, they are dust!

The Roman Centurion mentioned in Luke 7 had faith, he had admirable faith, Jesus marvelled when the Centurion demonstrated faith that is pure and based in how God operates, the centurion knew the chain of command from Heaven, where true authority comes from and how it should be delivered on earth.

When we grow up into Him there will be a mighty power working in us that exceeds all we could imagine or conjure up on earth.

A great reveal is coming.

There will be great exposure of the false gods.

Revealing what is truth and how we should live and move.

It is God who lives and moves in our beings.

His Glory will fill the earth.

Recently in April 2021, I heard in my spirit.

Legislation.

Game Changer.

Powerful legislation.

Someone said JUSTICE!

Just now in June 2021 I heard.
"I smell a rat!"
Referring to the Latest World Events and wicked
Global Governance.

The following is an Addendum to the chapter
about the *"Twelve Year old Miracle"*.
I am seeing a correlation to prophecies
previously declared.

The Asuza Street Revival where the Glory cloud
filled the meetings and miracles abounded that
attracted many from all over the world came to
an end in about 1909 – 1910 and both the
prominent leaders, Seymour and Parham
prophesised that in 100 years there would be an
even greater revival that would have far reaching
impact all over the world.

Also in 1913, another prominent revivalist Maria
Woodworth Eda prophesised that in 100 years
there would be a greater revival than the
outpourings she experienced where
unprecedented signs and wonders occurred and
the Holy Spirit moved freely filling the
atmosphere with the Glory, radically changing
lives in those meetings.

Do the Maths, add 100 years is 2009 - 2010 and
then we have the further date of 2013 which
puts us right in line with the birth and infancy
of this 12 year old child representing revival who
died and then was raised from dead.

We could also say the church was struggling to bring this revival into maturity, wrestling in faith for a breakthrough, represented by the woman who touched the hem of Jesus garment after 12 years of affliction, which is also the intensifying opposition from the enemy and the public that shunned her, viewing her present condition as unclean as stated by the law.

However, Obama came in to power in November 2008, things took a turn, the church started getting sick while in the process of birthing revival, the child was born but in amongst turmoil and great opposition. There is a spiritual battle going on here, the kingdom of darkness will do everything it can to stop the coming revival, wear down the saints, try to change times and seasons, every trick in the book but it is no match for the Almighty God we serve and in the end the battle is Gods and He will grind the mountain into dust to be scattered by the winds, obliterated.

Now here we are we just went through all of the events of 2020!
Now into 2021 and the fight is on!
Look at the current events and the laws that are introduced into our so called democracies opposing the Christian faith and meetings, masking everyone, keeping them quiet and contained in lockdowns, persecuting those that stand up to the tyranny and dare to question the fake totalitarian authority and then using the influence of the media to cancel cultures that don't fit their narrative.

This afflicted woman then got hold of Jesus like never before she suited up into the armour of God and took on the doubts, fears, disappointments, delays and distractions from the good health of destiny being fulfilled, she pressed through the crowd in faith expecting a miracle and received her healing. Sadly at the same time the afflicted woman was pressing through the crowd, the 12 year old girl representing revival had suffered a fatal blow.

The woman representing believers had persisted in faith through the crowd, even though she was considered to be illegal in the public places, cancelled and rejected by society.

However, the promises of God are Yes and Amen, the afflicted woman had the word of faith in her heart and nothing could stop her receiving the promised healing miracle and restoration. One touch from Jesus changed everything forever and then Jesus immediately went to where the dead girl was lying down. The crowd began mocking and questioning His actions, like they were saying *"we don't permit radical acts of faith here, just trust the science and the science gods persuasions on the masses"*, but then Jesus simply removed the sceptics outside, He then promptly raised that girl from the dead. Now the Church is restored and revival lives, Jesus is the Resurrection and the Life and nothing on this earth can stop the Glory, it is here now, smashing to pieces all of the stone idols of corrupt practices.

The knowledge of the Glory of God is filling the whole earth.
So we just add the twelve years of the restored church and the child called revival and we get 2021 – 2022 for a worldwide *Asuza Street Revival,* add another 4 years for *Maria Woodworth Eda* Signs and Wonders Revival, ok we get about 2025, could be another significant milestone in our progression of faith.

I also had a dream recently which I believe is relevant to our struggles.
The Dream about Accelerating Forward.
I am in a vehicle going backward erratically with my father driving struggling to gain control through a modern cityscape.
We are *"Going Backwards Fast."*
Things have been set in motion.
All forces just add up together building more momentum backwards.
We have ways of dealing with it, there is some control behind the wheel.
But we need to drive in reverse, not a good practice going fast in the streets of life.

We justify it, explain it, reason it, try to negotiate it!
We battle onwards using all of our driving old school methods.

That's the sense and the interpretation.
This lesson is about letting go of the old methods and practices and embracing the new which is true progressive faith.

Who is really in control behind the wheel in the driver's seat?
Do you get this drift?

Isaiah 35:8.
8 And an highway shall be there, and a way, and it shall be called The way of holiness; the unclean shall not pass over it; but it shall be for those: the wayfaring men, though fools, shall not err therein.

Again here is another addendum from the Chapter *"300"*.
To get to where Gideon's 300 became, in the progression from defeat to mighty men of valour where they trumped the enemy, there had to be a coming out of the place of being always under in defeat mode.
It started with Gideon from the place of fear and inferiority beginning to rise up and get those idols out of town, out of his life forever.
These were his father's idols, they were the limiting influence from inherited patterns of iniquity, they had to go or Gideon would never progress into a faith destiny.

Now I had another kind of visual impression dream. The what if? The *"Future City Dream"*.
I saw like billows of smoke and dark angry clouds thrashing around a city, with tornadoes funnelling down, it felt a bit like an apocalypse sci fi future city very modern skyscrapers and towers encapsulated by these ominous dark storm clouds.

There were dark clouds but the city was ultra-modern.
What if? The plans are achieved and there is no more freedom, only central control by the beast system!

It aint happening brothers and sisters, an army is rising, out of the ashes of the valley of clanging bones will arise a splendid array of willing soldiers like the dawn of a new day, progressing into brighter than the noonday sun.
Daniel 2
[41] And whereas thou sawest the feet and toes, part of potters' clay, and part of iron, the kingdom shall be divided; but there shall be in it of the strength of the iron, forasmuch as thou sawest the iron mixed with miry clay.
[42] And as the toes of the feet were part of iron, and part of clay, so the kingdom shall be partly strong, and partly broken.
[43] And whereas thou sawest iron mixed with miry clay, they shall mingle themselves with the seed of men: but they shall not cleave one to another, even as iron is not mixed with clay.
Daniel 2:33
His legs of iron, his feet part of iron and part of clay.

This final Kingdom is an insidious mixture of humanity with interdimensional entities that have infiltrated what is permissible by manipulation of Human DNA with alien technology, as described in Daniel 2, they mingled themselves with the seed of men.

These entities are operating in a similar practice to what occurred in the days of Noah, where fallen angels intermingled with women to produce the Nephilim hybrids.

How this will occur in the last days exactly is still in the making and we can only by research and insight predict these DNA manipulation practices.

With the addition of quantum computers and AI have provided a new means to globally influence and control minds taken captive by the spirit of the air. What about the particle accelerator? As in at the tower of Babel, whatever they put their minds to can be achieved, excepting for the restraints of the Most High and the end game of annihilation of these fallen creatures possessing advanced technologies.

Fallen Angels and demons are involved and they are using forbidden technology to bring about their plan to corrupt the seed of man in an attempt to thwart the end game by making humans into a hybrid being that is unredeemable. Satan driven by his megalomania and desperation to delay the inevitable judgement has the ultimate plan to stop the 2nd coming of Jesus Christ who will come back for a spotless bride the church. Satan in his desperation wants to remain on earth forever, creating a psycho hell on earth where mankind is recreated after his hideously corrupted image into a mixed up mingled DNA hybrid race that is forever doomed.

Remember if you take on Satan's characteristics that promises advancements in DNA human mental and physical capability, yes you will be superior and live longer but you will not be capable to love, you will just exist in a dark shadow with all of these super freak abilities and then finally the end will come and then you face the judgement into eternity.

The question is what is the mark of the beast? Well there are a lot of clues as elements are introduced in the lead up to the final temple of doom. Best to leave it alone and don't mess with it!

Notice in Daniel that the clay and iron do not cleave to one another, if we are somehow integrated into a part technology transhumanoid machine, this will cause distress to our souls, disturb our spirits and our body will reject such modification as unnatural, an impure and ugly thing, we would eventually implode and disintegrate.

However, that is the finality of things, where are we now on the timeline?

In a progression, just as faith is a progression, so it is with iniquity, it is a progression into a final doomsday. What is the opposite of the faith of God filling our temples? It is a possession of our beings by dark agendas with the false promise of being a demigod, this is the antichrist spirit that attempts to replace God with cleverly marketed counterfeits, conforming us to the pattern of a worldwide religion that appears noble on the surface, but will eventually destroy all of its members into hell.

However as sin abounds, grace abounds more.

There is more grace, in our weakness we are made strong by His overcoming grace.

There is the expression, *"feet of clay."* referring to a hidden fault or an unexpected flawed character within what should be of an expected reasonable standard.

Psalm 40:1,2 and 7,8.
I waited patiently for the LORD;
And He inclined to me,
And heard my cry.
2 He also brought me up out of a horrible pit,
Out of the miry clay,
And set my feet upon a rock,
And established my steps.

7 Then I said, "Behold, I come;
In the scroll of the book it is written of me.
8 I delight to do Your will, O my God,
And Your law is within my heart."

Mixtures can be a good thing or it can be detrimental to the character or the nature of the original form.
What has been happening ever since the fall is that we have a mixture of good and bad capabilities.
The thing is if something is presented to you and you know it is going to be a bad thing for you then you most likely won't accept it, unless there is some type of sugar coated candy reward offered or an attractive payment to accept the proposition.

People are bought, they are sold out to the offer they can't refuse, they sold their soul.
This particularly refers to people in positions of influence and power, Government Officials, Government Leaders, Law Enforcement Agents, Judges and the judicial system and the like.
Now they also can be intimidated and manipulated by fear if they won't accept the offer initially or resist.

Decline into the miry clay is usually a process, takes time with plotting and scheming by the fowler setting the trap to lure its victims, using any means available to entice and eventually compel us as flawed people into the pit as we are trying to find our way and make sense of this world.

The Good News is we can all find our expression in the progression, from our feet being embedded in the miry clay to where we are delivered by His grace out of a horrible pit to where our character is refined to the expression *"I delight to do your will."*

In this world we are like Jesus.

As He is so are we.

There is the hidden dangers in mixtures into our faith that we need to be aware of, like the Laodecian Church, things crept into their faith. They may have undealt with issues that resulted in an eventual decline into compromise.

The thing with harmful mixtures is they are packaged well, they can be appealing to our unrefined carnal natures and this is where we need to progress our faith as these things surface and come into the light, we can choose to submit to the refining process, put off the old nature, put to death the deeds of the flesh by the prompting by the Holy Spirit leading us into the Highway of Holiness.

Impure mixtures are harder to discern as they appear to be something we can add into our lives without any consequences, it seems like a good blend.

We don't want any harmful mixtures blending into our faith, they creep into in phases over a long period of time like a dripping tap watering down our faith like a muddy seepage into churches and believers lives that hinder the faith.

The enemy uses slow infiltration a sneaky bit at a time of mixed in philosophies, worldly beliefs and practices.

We should earnestly contend for the faith which was once delivered unto the saints as in the Book of Jude there was a stern warning to the saints of God of the evil plans of the enemy to infiltrate the church with corruption leading to destruction.

Until he reaches his goal of corruption and compromise loss of power and authority then destruction.

Wow what an eventful night it was on the 26th May 2021 after 40 years a rare blood super moon appeared in the night sky in New Zealand and the peak time of this rare phenomena was 11:11pm where the total eclipse occurred with a blood red moon spectacle that also displayed like a halo flare on the perimeter of the super moon.

Fascinating days! I experienced this blood moon that night, what a spectacular show.
11:11pm was the time to reach fullness that seems to point to a significant symbolic time on the divine timetable. Stay in tune.

Haggai 2
6 "For thus says the LORD of hosts: 'Once more (it is a little while) I will shake heaven and earth, the sea and dry land;
7 and I will shake all nations, and they shall come to the Desire of All Nations, and I will fill this temple with glory,' says the LORD of hosts.
8 'The silver is Mine, and the gold is Mine,' says the LORD of hosts.
9 'The glory of this latter temple shall be greater than the former,' says the LORD of hosts. 'And in this place I will give peace,' says the LORD of hosts."
Stay in tune, there is a lot of shaking going on spoken by the prophet Haggai, as well as many prophets in this day.

Shaking removes and separates the impure from the pure.
Shaking can be part of the refining process.

Sifting to bring out the gold when in a mixture together with other shiny particles, they may all look much the same, but they are vastly different in nature and composition. Gold mining involves a process where the particles that don't have the same pure properties as gold need to be separated, so that only the gold that is of great worth remains.

Haggai 2
21 "Speak to Zerubbabel, governor of Judah, saying:
'I will shake heaven and earth.
22 I will overthrow the throne of kingdoms;
I will destroy the strength of the Gentile kingdoms.
I will overthrow the chariots
And those who ride in them;
The horses and their riders shall come down,
Every one by the sword of his brother.

They say you can discern the times, when you look into the sky and see certain signs that point to a coming significant event.
This where we need our spiritual eyes tuned to see what is coming and what we need to be aware of and prepare ourselves, ask for wisdom and He will direct our paths.

The church is not left as abandoned orphans on planet earth to fight it out alone, on the contrary we have been given authority from Heaven and weapons of warfare to contend for the faith.

We can speak peace to the storms.

Isaiah 41
15 Behold, I will make thee a new sharp threshing instrument having teeth: thou shalt thresh the mountains, and beat them small, and shalt make the hills as chaff.
16 Thou shalt fan them, and the wind shall carry them away, and the whirlwind shall scatter them: and thou shalt rejoice in the LORD, and shalt glory in the Holy One of Israel.

Words have the power to dissolve matter rearranging the composition of the framework and elements of our physical world to the atomic levels, words will shift the atmosphere to remove the forces that hold like a concrete wall that surrounds us, containing us in a confined space.

When we speak the Word of God that has been given to us, we can grind the walls of oppression down into tiny particles that become dust in the wind.

More that we can imagine happens, more than we could ever conceive is effected down to the atomic structures in the fabric of our physical world. We change the state of our home, neighbourhood, communities, nation and the world as directed.

Our words carry substance and like light rays shooting forth directed at a target it will create change for the better or for the worse.

Life and death are in the power of the tongue.

When we are aligned with Gods ways then our words carry weight in the spiritual realms and what we speak into the atmosphere, what we decree and declare, what we issue as a prayer of command to change the atmosphere will bring Gods Kingdom into the earth in the domain of humanity.

Jesus has all authority and He gives His authority to the church which is His Body of believers, following Him and obeying His commands. We take dominion, sin no longer has dominion over us.

We have not being given a spirit of fear.
Perfect love drives out fear.
We have been given the spirit of power love and sound mind, this is the heart motivation of our faith that changes our world for the better. We guard our hearts for out of a healthy heart comes our vibrant springs of life.

Fear is a debilitating tool of the enemy and it gets our focus off faith onto the driving force of fear as the engine taking us backwards fast. Fear is the fuel that drives us backwards fast and then faster, to scaringly faster to the point where we can barely control where we are heading and what is coming at us. Is the Holy Spirit at the steering wheel of our life or is it our emotions and wrestling at the oars to get to the other side? It takes faith to trust that Father God is our driver, I know we could easily say Jesus is at the wheel as well, either way God is One and He has got this.

When we experience His love and take hold of the truth that nothing in this world or the second heaven hordes of influences can separate us from the love of God. How do we shift gears from backwards in fear to forwards in faith? It is a journey, a progression beginning with baby steps to mature choices, if you are up against it, the wind and the storms are thrashing around you driving you back for cover, it is not over, the battle has just began and you will come out of this experience a different person, stronger and wiser, learning to put your trust in God, no longer leaning on your own understanding for solutions, not driven by generational habits and patterns of behaviour, you will put on Christ, the new man and woman of faith, the hope of Glory is Christ in us, our new day is arising brighter each day.

"I can see, I can see clearly now, things look so different from this perspective, I can see beyond , seeing beyond 2020 vision, seeing beyond the trials and tribulations, knowing the love that passes understanding, I am accepted in the beloved and I can overcome this crazy world."

Proverbs 3
7 Be not wise in thine own eyes: fear the LORD, and depart from evil.

What is pride? What is false humility?

Settling for less than God called you to be, or striving to be more than God called you to be.

275

Being out of your place that God ordained for you to be in, which is your God given sphere of influence, the good works He predestined you to walk in, you serve there in the gifts and capacity as well as the measure of faith that is graced to you to be and do in all of the days apportioned for you to live in.

Remember faith expresses itself by love, so our character is also aligned to be as He is, we find love, joy and peace when we enter into His rest and take His yoke upon us, all these things are added to us. He makes the path of life known to us and in His presence is fullness of joy and pleasures forevermore. *Psalm 16.*

God wants us made whole.
Wholeness is being complete in our spirit, soul and body.
It is about the whole man being sanctified, purified to be as He is in this world.
God doesn't want a mixture of beliefs in our soul, soul ties, soul wounds, fear triggers and the lust for the things of this world.
God wants our faith to be free from hindrances that will stunt our growth, It is His will that we prosper and be in health as our soul prospers.
We have an inheritance as His sons and daughters and He doesn't want us to be robbed of this.
Where is our victory? Our faith overcomes and we are no longer conformed to the patterns of this world mixed into our beings.
The Glory of God is here. The Glory is progressively filling the earth.

This is the prayer of Jesus for the believers from *John 17, "And the glory which You gave Me I have given them, that they may be one just as We are one."*

Seeing beyond 2020 vision is not a natural point of view, it takes you beyond your usual perceptions projected by the influencing voices that are the dark web cloud blanketing the earth. Seeing beyond positions you above where you will mount up with wings like eagles into the higher realms, where all things are possible for the future.

Also don't forget
I have three eBooks available for more with
similar content and messages.
Must Read!!!
Grace Be Grace Do
Brother! You Didn't Earn it!
Walk the Talk on Hot Coals
Go to my website for details about where to get
these.
http://www.beinginthelight.com/ebooks.html

*The time of the writing of the first release of the
book was mid October 2020, prior to the coming
USA election. Since then chapters have been
added as the vision progressed, which has not
changed this vision but rather added more
content to it for the readers benefit.*

I am in His service as a scribe writing down the
thoughts that come to me in my own
unique expression.
To God be the Glory for the good things He has
done and will be doing in our bright future.

Cover design and illustrations by Peter Koren
Initial graphics layout contributions
by sam_4321 on Fiveer
300 Illustration by Krkoska aka Peter Koren
Black and White Artwork Design by Peter Koren
Vector lines vectorperfector on Fiveer